Reproducible Activities

Theme-Based
Reading Comprehension

Grade 3

Published by Instructional Fair • TS Denison
an imprint of

Author: Margaret Fetty
Editor: Sara Bierling

 Children's Publishing

Published by Instructional Fair • TS Denison
An imprint of McGraw-Hill Children's Publishing
Copyright © 2004 McGraw-Hill Children's Publishing

Limited Reproduction Permission: Permission to duplicate these materials is limited to the person for whom they are purchased. Reproduction for an entire school or school district is unlawful and strictly prohibited.

All Rights Reserved • Printed in the United States of America

Send all inquiries to:
McGraw-Hill Children's Publishing
3195 Wilson Drive NW
Grand Rapids, Michigan 49544

Theme-Based Reading Comprehension—grade 3
ISBN: 0-7424-1923-1

1 2 3 4 5 6 7 8 MAL 09 08 07 06 05 04

The McGraw-Hill Companies

Table of Contents

Introduction 5
Cross-Curricular Correlation Chart 6
Standards Correlation Chart 7
Pretest 8
Posttest 9

Plants
Plant Cycles 10
Tree Needs 11–12
Memory Tree 13
A "Berry" Colorful Dye 14
The Kite-Eating Tree 15
From Forest to House 16
Petal Patterns....................................17–18
A Japanese Art 19
Thank You, Mr. Carver!..........................20

The Solar System
Moon Festival...21
Oh, Mister Moon 22
It's Just a Phase 23–24
The Science Test 25–26
Size Counts...27
A Postcard from Rome..........................28
On a Moonwalk 29
Going in Circles 30
The North Star 31
Out in Space 32
All in a Year 33

The Middle Ages
I Want to Be a Knight 34
Tool Time..35–36
The Farming Life 37
Castles 38
Catherine Helps 39
A Farming Experiment 40
What Fun!..41
This Is an Acre 42
Marco Polo Returns..........................43–44
Join a Guild 45

The West
Children Help, Too 46
Landforms on the Oregon Trail 47–48
You're Invited to a House Raising....49–50
Johnnycakes 51
Packing for the Trip...............................52
Kitchen Music 53
Problems on the Plains 54
Life in a Desert 55–56
Pioneer Troubles 57–58
A Cloth Picture 59–60

Pets
Why Animals Can't Talk 61–62
Pookie's Walk......................................63–64
Caring for Speckles................................65
Aquarium Competition 66
Small, Medium, and Large Dogs...........67
An Unusual Pet 68
Pet Survey 69–70
Pet Pictures 71
The Speech 72

Table of Contents

Architecture
Three-Dimensional Buildings..............73–74
Snow Today, Water Tomorrow! 75
Building Artists 76
Kinds of Houses 77
House Patterns..................................78
The Japanese House 79
That's Electricity................................80

Family
Julie's Budget 81
Time to Vote 82
Growing Up 83
The Family Portrait.............................84
Happy Kwanzaa! 85
David Goes to Work 86
The Totem Pole 87
A Family 88
Mr. Nobody 89

Community
Many Kinds of Communities 90
An Ant Community.............................91
It's the Law......................................92
A Chain of Life 93–94
Community Fun.................................95
Vacation Weather 96
The Mural Contest..............................97
Communities Here and There 98

Seasons
Why Bears Hibernate in Winter:
  A Native-American Folktale..........99–100
The March Wind 101
How Far Away?................................102
Make a Tornado 103
Ellie's Favorite Season........................104
Animals Adapt.................................105
Monsoon Winds...............................106
The Climate Seasons 107
Gung Hay Fat Choy! 108

Insects
Insects—One Big Happy Group 109
Insect Record Holders 110
Silk-Screen Prints 111
Big Bugs 112
Butterfly Lessons..............................113
A New Kind of Thermometer 114
A Butterfly Life Cycle.........................115
The Legend of Silk 116
Working to Save
  the Monarch Butterfly......................117

Answer Key.................................118–128

Introduction

With the increased focus on literacy in the classroom, it is more important than ever to provide students with interesting reading activities. These reading activities should help develop students' phonemic awareness, phonics skills, fluency, vocabulary, and comprehension. Students should also be regularly assessed on their reading comprehension skills. Frequent assessment by the instructor prevents the reinforcement of flawed comprehension skills.

This book has been written thematically. Each of the ten themes has seven to eleven reading selections. The use of themes increases reading comprehension skills by focusing students' attention on one subject rather than asking students to adjust their thoughts to several subjects. Use the pages located within each theme as a unit or individually at different times throughout the school year. Pages are independent and do not need to be completed as whole theme units.

The themes included in this book are Plants, The Solar System, The Middle Ages, The West, Pets, Architecture, Family, Community, Seasons, and Insects. The thematic reading selections include fiction, nonfiction, recipes, graphs, biographies, and poetry. The activities reinforce comprehension skills such as finding the main idea, summarizing, inferencing, cloze procedure, compare and contrast, sequencing, cause and effect, story elements, and classification. The activities include a variety of multiple choice, fill-in-the-blank, short answer, and long answer questions.

A standards correlation chart has been included for your convenience. Use this chart as a checklist for your students' skills. Regularly refer to this chart to keep the skills fresh in your mind. Slowly introduce students to the language used in these standards. A pretest and posttest are also included to further facilitate the assessment process.

Cross-Curricular Correlation Chart

	Language Arts	Math	Social Studies	Science	Arts
Plants	13	14, 15, 17–18	16	10, 11–12, 20	14, 19
The Solar System	22	23–24, 27, 33	21, 32	23–24, 25–26, 29, 30, 31, 33	28
The Middle Ages		42	34, 37, 38, 43–44, 45	35–36, 40	39, 41
The West	61–62	49–50, 51, 52	46, 54, 57–58,	47–48, 49–50, 55–56	53, 59–60
Pets		63–64, 67, 69–70	61–62	65, 66, 68, 72	71
Architecture		73–74, 78	77, 79, 82	75, 80	76
Family	89	81, 86	82, 83, 85, 88		84, 87
Community		96	90, 92, 97, 98	91, 93–94	95, 97
Seasons	99–100, 101	102	99–100, 104, 108	102, 103, 105, 106, 107	
Insects	116	110, 113, 114	116, 117	109, 110, 112, 113, 115	111

© McGraw-Hill Children's Publishing

0-7424-1923-1 Theme-Based Reading Comprehension

Standards Correlation Chart

Sample Standards	*CAT Level 31	**CTBS Level 31
Reading		
Vocabulary		
Using Synonyms	X	X
Using Antonyms	X	X
Using Homophones		
Using Homographs		
Using Multi-Meaning Words		
Using Context Clues	X	X
Using Prefixes and Suffixes		
Comprehension		
Identifying Main Idea	X	X
Identifying Supporting Details	X	X
Identifying Sequence of Events	X	X
Drawing Conclusions	X	X
Making Predictions	X	X
Comparing and Contrasting	X	X
Identifying Cause and Effect	X	X
Identifying Character Traits/Feelings	X	X
Identifying Story Parts	X	
Distinguishing Between Fact and Opinion	X	
Using Graphic Organizers	X	X
Summarizing	X	X
Identifying Author's Purpose	X	X
Reading Various Genres	X	X
Language		
Mechanics Expression		
Using Correct Capitalization and Punctuation	X	X
Determining Correct Usage	X	X
Recognizing Sentence Structures	X	X
Combining Sentence	X	
Using Simple and Compound Sentences		
Identifying Topic Sentences for Paragraphs		X
Identifying Supporting Sentences for Paragraphs		X
Spelling		
Identifying Correct Spelling		X
Identifying Incorrect Spelling		X

* CAT 11 Terra Nova CAT™ ©2001 CTB/McGraw-Hill
** CTBS 11 Terra Nova CTBS® ©1997 CTB/McGraw-Hill

Pretest Name _____ Date _____

The Lion and the Boar
by Aesop

In the heat of the summer sun, Lion went to a small watering hole to get a drink of cool water. As he walked out of the grass, he saw Boar walking toward the water. At the same time, Boar saw Lion and rushed to be first to the water. Both animals got there at the same time and began to argue.

"I will go first," said Lion. "I am the king of the jungle."

Boar shook his head and smiled widely to show Lion his long teeth. "But Lion, I should drink first because I come here at this time every day."

The two animals raised their voices. Lion shook his heavy paw, and Boar stomped his big hoof as they talked. Lion was tired of arguing. He raised his head and let out a roar. He was ready to fight. But as Lion looked up, he saw vultures flying above.

He pointed to the sky and said, "Boar, the vultures are hungry. They want one of us to get hurt."

"Then let's find a way to agree on the problem," said Boar. "If we are friends, the vultures will have to go somewhere else. I think it is better to solve our problems now and face this danger together."

The two animals agreed on a plan. Lion would drink each morning, and Boar would drink each night.

1. Why were the animals arguing? _____

2. Why do you think Boar showed his teeth when he smiled? _____

3. What happened after Lion roared? _____

4. What might have happened if Lion and Boar did not find a way to solve the problem? _____

Natural Friends

The acacia tree grows in the grasslands of Africa. Ants usually make their homes in the branches of the tree. The acacia and the ants form a friendship that helps both of them survive the hot, dry summers in Africa.

The acacia tree has a special sugar in its leaves. The ants feed on the tasty leaves for food. The ants also get water from the leaves.

The ants help the tree in return. They clear out the grass that grows near the trunk. The grass uses the water that the tree needs to survive during the summer. Also, the ants sting animals that try to eat the bark or leaves of the acacia tree. Giraffes enjoy munching the leaves on the acacia tree. Like the ants, they enjoy the sweet taste. But the giraffes don't stay too long at one tree. The ants swarm and bite the giraffes to make them leave.

1. What is this story mostly about? _____

2. How does the acacia tree help the ant? _____

3. How does the ant help the acacia tree? _____

4. What might happen if an acacia tree did not have ants to help it? _____

Science   Name _____   Date _____

Plant Cycles

All living things have life cycles. A cycle is something that happens over and over again. A life cycle is the birth, growth, and death of a living thing. A plant is a living thing, so it has a life cycle.

You can see a life cycle if you plant some seeds in dirt. With water and sunshine, the plant begins to grow. At first, you will not see anything happen. But under the ground, the seed is changing. First, it grows a root. Then a shoot with leaves begins to grow. In a few more days, a seedling will grow out of the ground, and the leaves will spread out. Soon it will grow into a green plant with a long stem and many leaves.

Then one day you will notice a bud. The flower petals are closed tightly inside the bud. It opens a little each day until it forms a beautiful flower. The flower seeds are inside the flower where the stem and flower meet.

Most flowers do not live very long. They turn brown and fall to the ground. The seeds are left on the stem. The wind blows the seeds to the ground, or an animal helps spread the seeds by carrying them to other places. But once the seeds are on the ground, they are ready to start the life cycle all over again.

Directions: Use words from the story to complete the sentences.

1. A _____ is something that happens over and over again.

2. A seedling has a _____ with a few leaves.

3. The _____ contains tightly-closed flower petals.

4. During the last part of a plant's life cycle, the _____ forms.

Science   Name _____   Date _____

Tree Needs

Directions: Read the story. Then answer the questions on page 12.

Dave was helping his dad plant some small ash trees in the yard. He pushed the dirt around the base of one tree. Then he stood up and wiped his brow.

"Two trees planted and one more to go!" said Mr. Ruiz.

Dave picked up the shovel and walked over to the place where they had laid out the last tree. He pushed the shovel into the ground. The point wouldn't go in, so Dave tried jumping on the shovel.

"Dad, the ground here is so hard I can't get the blade in the soil," said Dave.

Mr. Ruiz came and looked at the ground. "We may need to find another place to plant this tree," he said. "Like all plants, trees need four things—sunlight, air, water, and good soil. While there is plenty of sunlight, this place may lack the soil, water, and air that the tree needs."

Dave looked puzzled. "We water the plants, and there's air all around us. This tree will have plenty of water and air," he said.

"We may water the plants, but the water drains into the soil and forms little pockets. The air does the same thing. If the soil is hard or rocky, the air and water cannot get into the ground," answered Mr. Ruiz.

As Mr. Ruiz talked, he slowly walked around the yard. Every once in a while, he poked the point of the shovel into the dirt to test the soil. "The water, air, and soil have vitamins that plants need to make them healthy. The roots are the parts of the plant that take in the nutrients. If the roots can't get the nutrients they need, the plant won't grow very well. It won't be healthy."

Soon the shovel blade sliced easily into the dirt. "I think we just found a new home for this last tree," said Mr. Ruiz. "Do you see this soil? It's loose and black, which means there are lots of nutrients in it. And with the soil being loose, the water and air can easily drain down to the tree's roots."

"Well, let's hurry and finish planting this tree because I'm getting hungry. If I don't get some nutrients soon, I might not grow either," laughed Dave.

© McGraw-Hill Children's Publishing   11   0-7424-1923-1 *Theme-Based Reading Comprehension*

Science   Name _____   Date _____

Tree Needs (cont.)

1. What four things does a plant need to grow? _____
_____

2. Why do you think Dave couldn't get the shovel in the ground?
_____
_____

3. What are two ways plants get water? _____
_____

4. What part of a plant takes in water and air?
_____

5. Why can't air and water drain into soil that is hard? _____
_____

6. What did Dave mean at the end of the story when he said he needed nutrients? _____
_____

© McGraw-Hill Children's Publishing   0-7424-1923-1 Theme-Based Reading Comprehension

Language Arts   Name _____   Date _____

Memory Tree

I have planted a memory tree,
neither too great
nor too small.
A tree for life—
to celebrate the beauty around me
and to remind me.

May this tree of life I have set to earth
grow roots strongly anchored,
grow branches stretching wide,
to remind me often
of a grandparent's arms
and that loving embrace.

1. What summarizes this poet's message?
   a. Trees grow strong and wide when planted correctly.
   b. The poet loves to sit under trees and remember things.
   c. The poet plants a tree to celebrate Earth Day.
   d. The poet plants a tree to help her deal with missing a grandparent.

2. What does the poet remember?
   a. how to plant a tree
   b. trees she has planted in the past
   c. her grandparent's love
   d. that trees have strong roots and branches

3. What is the poet celebrating?
   a. the beauty of the world and love
   b. trees
   c. Earth Day
   d. memories

© McGraw-Hill Children's Publishing   13   0-7424-1923-1 Theme-Based Reading Comprehension

Arts/Math Name _____ Date_____

A "Berry" Colorful Dye

People have always used different parts of plants to make dyes. Some people still dye their own cloth. Here is a recipe you can try. Ask an adult to help you. Then follow this recipe to make a "berry" colorful dye.

BERRY DYE
Yield: Enough dye to color 1 lb. of wool or cotton cloth
1 lb. (.5 kg) berries, 4 gal. (15 L) water, knife, large pot, strainer
1. Chop the berries.
2. Place the berries and water in a pot.
3. Bring the water and berries to a boil.
4. Turn down the heat to low. Simmer the mixture for 30 to 60 minutes. The color will be deeper when the mixture is heated for a longer time.
5. Strain out the berry pieces.
6. Cool the dye.

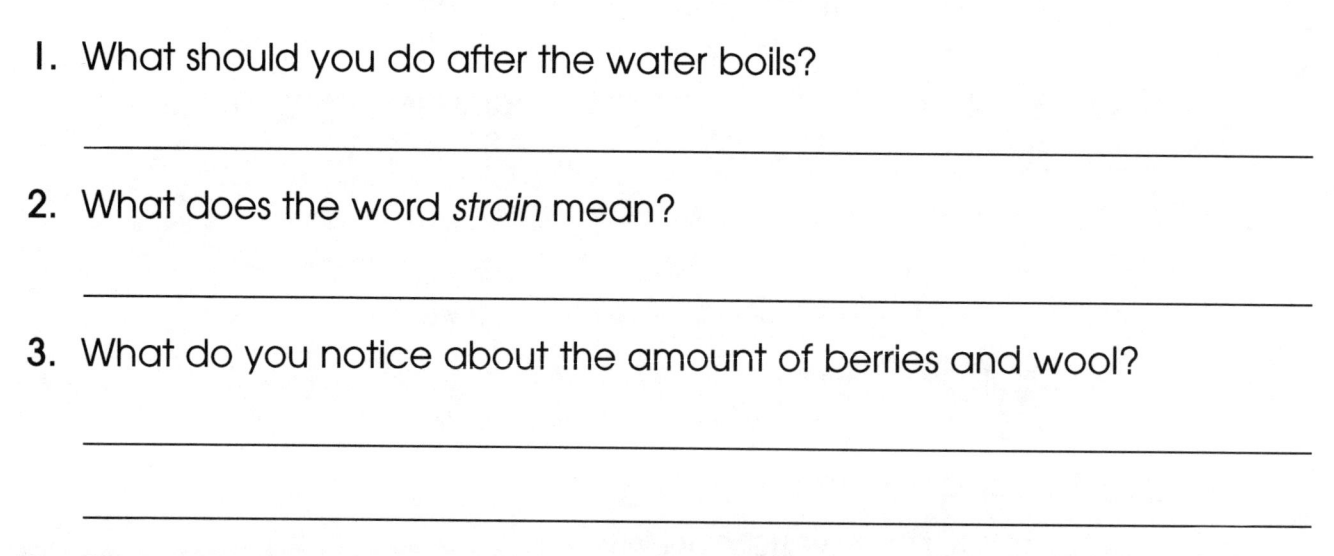

---

1. What should you do after the water boils?
   _____

2. What does the word *strain* mean?
   _____

3. What do you notice about the amount of berries and wool?
   _____
   _____

4. If you wanted to double the batch of dye, how many berries and how much water would you need?
   _____

Math   Name _____   Date _____

The Kite-Eating Tree

Manny crossed his arms and looked up in the tree. "Another kite eaten by the tree," he muttered.

"My dad has a 24-foot ladder. If we knew how tall the tree was, we might be able to use it to get the kite," said Kate.

"Hey, that's a great idea!" shouted Manny. "Let's find out how tall this tree is. We did something like this in math class. We measured a stick and its shadow, and then we measured the shadow of a tree. We used equivalent fractions to calculate the height of a tree."

"That's right!" exclaimed Kate. "You go get a tape measure, and I'll find a short tree. We can measure a little tree and its shadow the same way we measured the stick."

When Manny came back, he had a tape measure, some paper, and a pencil. Kate stood beside a short pine tree. The two friends quickly set to work. They found that the height of the short tree was 4 feet tall. Its shadow was 6 feet tall. When Manny and Kate measured the shadow of the tree holding the kite, they found that its shadow was 30 feet long.

Manny quickly wrote an equation with fractions using the measurements from the trees: $\frac{4}{6} = \frac{x}{30}$.

After Manny worked the problem, he yelled, "The tree is 20 feet tall! Your dad's ladder will reach up that high!"

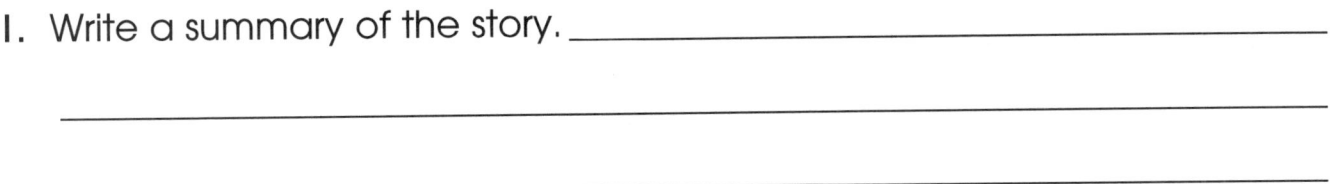

1. Write a summary of the story. _____

_____

2. What did Kate do while Manny went to get the tape measure?

_____

3. Show how Manny solved the equation using fractions to find the height of the tree.

4. Where do you think Manny and Kate will fly the kite next time?

_____

Social Studies   Name _____   Date _____

From Forest to House

Dear Chau,

We are having a wonderful vacation. Right now we are in Oregon visiting my uncle. He works at a sawmill. Loggers choose a place to cut down a tree. They must be careful so the tree won't get caught on another tree. Then the loggers make cuts on the trunk with axes and chain saws. Sometimes they use large saws to cut the trees. Once the trees are down, a large machine with a claw hauls the trees to trucks. Then the trucks take the trees to a sawmill.

At the sawmill, the bark is removed. The tree is sawed along the whole length into long square blocks. Another machine cuts the blocks into strips of lumber. The strips are very rough. The next machine, called a planing machine, makes them smooth all around. Now the lumber looks like the boards we used to build our tree house.

Finally, the boards are put into a kiln. My uncle says that if the wood is not dried out, the boards will twist and crack when they are nailed together. Sometimes the wood is left outside to dry, but it takes several months before the wood can be used.

Wow! I never knew so much was needed to turn a tree into a house.

I'll be home soon. Then I'll show you my pictures.

Love,
Marcy

1. What might happen if a tree gets caught on another tree as it falls?
   _____

2. What happens after the bark is cut off the trees? _____
   _____

3. What does a kiln do? _____

4. What happens if the wood is not dried? _____
   _____

Petal Patterns

Directions: Read the article. Then answer the questions on page 18.

Patterns are all around us. Some patterns are made by people. You can see patterns in the shapes of buildings and in colors of clothing. There are many patterns in nature, too. Did you know that flowers have patterns? Few people know that flower petals follow a number pattern. This number pattern is called the Fibonacci sequence.

Leonardo Fibonacci (fib ohn AH chee) was born in Italy around 1175. He studied numbers and nature. Fibonacci found that one number pattern was repeated in plants and animals. In the Fibonacci sequence, a group of numbers are added the same way to make a pattern. The pattern is as follows: 1, 1, 2, 3, 5, 8, 13, 21, 34, 55, 89, 144 ...

The pattern is made by adding the two numbers before to find the sum of the next number:

1 + 1 = 2
1 + 2 = 3
2 + 3 = 5, and so on

So how does the Fibonacci sequence make a pattern in flowers? The number of petals on a flower is a number in the pattern. The next time you are outside, find a flower. Carefully count the petals. You will be amazed with this pattern in nature.

Math　　Name _____　　Date_____

Petal Patterns (cont.)

1. What is a pattern? _____
   _____

2. Who was Leonardo Fibonacci? _____
   _____

3. The last number given in the Fibonacci sequence is 144. What number comes next? Show your work.

4. Which sentence from the article is an opinion? Circle it.

   There are many patterns in nature, too.

   You will be amazed with this pattern in nature.

5. Leaves also have patterns. Look at the leaf below.

   Describe two patterns that you see. _____
   _____
   _____

Arts Name _____ Date _____

A Japanese Art

Ikebana is the art of arranging flowers. It is a fun art that people in Japan learn. Ikebana is many centuries old. It started in China. Monks made beautiful flower arrangements to give to Buddha, their god. Some of the monks traveled to Japan. Over time, the people in Japan saw the flowers the monks arranged. They liked the simple beauty. The Japanese people turned it into an art.

Ikebana arrangements are made of things from nature. Each arrangement must use flowers, leaves, and twigs. But the goal of ikebana is for the beauty of each flower to show. That is why ikebana uses very few flowers or stems.

Ikebana may look simple, but there are many rules to learn. People go to school to learn these rules. Once a student is done, he or she is an ikebana master. Masters know exactly how tall the flowers and twigs should be. They also know how to position the flowers. The arrangements are not symmetrical. They look uneven. A twig may stick out on one side of the arrangement with no flower or twig to balance it on the other side. Once done, the arrangement is set in a place of honor for all to enjoy.

1. What is ikebana?
    a. growing flowers
    b. arranging flowers
    c. cooking with flowers
    d. planting flowers

2. Ikebana arrangements are simple because
    a. there are not many flowers in Japan.
    b. the arrangements must be uneven.
    c. the beauty of each flower must show.
    d. people do not know what they are doing.

3. What happened when monks came to Japan?
    a. They shared the secrets of ikebana.
    b. They learned about ikebana.
    c. They gave flowers to Buddha.
    d. They grew flowers.

4. How does the author feel about ikebana?
    a. She thinks the arrangements are too simple.
    b. She does not like this kind of art.
    c. She thinks it is hard to learn.
    d. She likes the arrangements.

Science   Name   Date

Thank You, Mr. Carver!

What do cherry punch, peanut butter, paint, and shoe polish have in common? They can be made from the peanut plant! Moreover, one man—George Washington Carver—found that peanuts could be used to make these goods.

George Washington Carver was born a slave in 1864. Carver was very curious. He wanted to learn. He taught himself to read and write. Carver heard about a school for African-American students. The school was eight miles away. Carver walked to and from school each day.

Carver was able to go to a college in Iowa. He decided he wanted to help farmers in the South. He experimented with different plants to find ones that would make the soil better. Carver found that the peanut plant helped the soil.

Carver traveled all over the South telling farmers about peanuts. The farmers did not want to grow peanuts. No one would buy peanuts from farmers. The farmers could not make any money. So Carver began to find new uses for peanuts. Carver used peanuts to make foods such as punch, pimento cheese, coffee, and flour. He also found that the little peanut could be used to make many other goods. Among his discoveries were shampoo, car grease, soap, rubber, and wood filler. In all, Carver found over 300 ways to use the peanut plant.

1. Which product is NOT made from peanuts?
   a. paint
   b. shampoo
   c. mustard
   d. punch

2. Farmers would not grow peanuts at first because ...
   a. there were few uses for peanuts.
   b. peanuts would not grow in poor soil.
   c. peanuts cost too much.
   d. no one ate pimento cheese.

3. What could be another title for this article?
   a. The Peanut Man
   b. Good Foods
   c. From Farm to Table
   d. How to Make Better Soil

4. The author wrote this article
   a. to get you to buy peanuts.
   b. to tell about the man who helped farmers.
   c. to tell a make-believe story.
   d. to tell how to grow peanuts.

Social Studies   Name _____   Date _____

Moon Festival

Dear Anne,

Please join my family and me for the Moon Festival. It's the biggest holiday in China. It always takes place on August 15. That is when the moon is the biggest and the brightest.

The holiday is very much like the American holiday of Thanksgiving. We celebrate the end of the harvest. Family and friends get together, and we have a big feast. Instead of apple pie for dessert, we eat moon cakes. Moon cakes are small cakes that are about the size of a hand. They are filled with nuts and dates. Sometimes people hide the hard yolk of an egg inside. The round yolk looks like the moon.

On Moon Festival night, all of the children get to stay up late. Everyone watches the full moon rise in the sky. We listen to poems and songs about the moon.

It will be great fun. I hope you can come.

Your friend,
Soon-Li

1. When does the Moon Festival take place? _____

2. What country celebrates the Moon Festival? _____

3. When do the people listen to poems and songs? _____

4. Name three ways the Moon Festival is like the American holiday of Thanksgiving. _____

Oh, Mister Moon

Oh, Mister Moon, Moon,
Bright and shiny moon,
Won't you please shine
down on me.

Oh, Mister Moon, Moon,
Bright and shiny moon,
Hiding behind that tree.

I'd like to stay,
But I've got to run.

There's a new day coming
With the morning sun.

Oh, Mister Moon, Moon,
Bright and shiny moon,
Won't you please shine
down on me.

1. What time of day is it? _____

2. What do you think the moon in the song looks like? Tell why you think so.
   _____
   _____

3. Why do you think the moon is hiding behind the tree? _____
   _____
   _____

4. Where might the person in the song be going?
   _____

It's Just a Phase

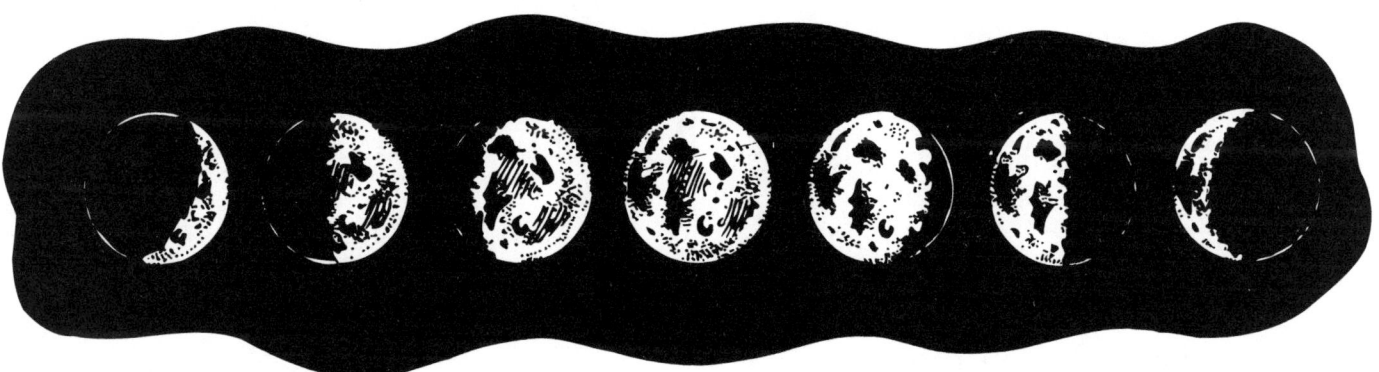

Directions: Read the article. Then answers the questions on page 24.

The moon is the largest object in the sky at night. The light from the moon is caused by light that is reflected from the sun.

Just like the earth orbits around the sun, the moon circles around the earth. It takes about 29 days for the moon to make one full circle. Sometimes it looks like a big full circle, and other times it looks like a thin sliver. These different shapes are called phases.

When the moon begins its orbit, it is between the sun and the earth. The sun shines on the side of the moon that faces it, while the side facing earth is dark. Since the moon is at the beginning of its cycle, this phase is called the new moon.

At the end of one week, the moon has completed one-fourth of its orbit. This phase of the orbit is called the first quarter moon. During this time, the sun shines on half of the moon's surface. The moon looks like a half circle.

As the orbit continues, more and more of the moon can be seen. At the end of two weeks, there is a full moon. During this phase, Earth is between the sun and the moon. The sun shines on the moon to make it look like a full circle. The moon's orbit is halfway complete.

By the third week, the moon has finished three-quarters of its orbit. Only half of it can be seen again. This phase is known as the last quarter moon. By the end of the fourth week, the moon has made one full orbit. It is once again in a new moon phase.

Science/Math   Name _____   Date_____

It's Just a Phase (cont.)

1. What is the effect of the sun shining on the moon?
   a. The moon looks as though it glows.
   b. The moon orbits Earth.
   c. The moon changes shape.
   d. The moon orbits the sun.

2. What does *reflect* mean?
   a. to see
   b. to glow
   c. to orbit
   d. to bounce back

3. Which of these is not a phase of the moon?
   a. full moon
   b. new moon
   c. silver moon
   d. first quarter

4. About how many days have passed when the moon completes one-half of its orbit.
   a. 7
   b. 14
   c. 21
   d. 28

5. How much of the moon can be seen during the last quarter phase?
   a. $\frac{1}{8}$
   b. $\frac{1}{4}$
   c. $\frac{1}{2}$
   d. $\frac{3}{4}$

6. What does the moon look like at the end of the fourth week?
   a. It is dark.
   b. It looks like a big circle.
   c. It looks like a sliver.
   d. It looks like a half circle.

Science   Name _____   Date _____

The Science Test

Direction: Read the story. Then answer the questions on page 26.

The big science test was tomorrow. The test was about the solar system. Wes was ready for the test—except for one problem. He could not remember the names of the planets in order.

Wes knew the teacher would give the class a picture of the solar system. The students would be asked to write the names of the planets. Some planets would be easy to name. He knew Mercury, Earth, and Pluto. But how would Wes remember the other six planets?

Wes's sister looked in his room. "You are looking worried," Keisha said. "What's wrong?"

"I have this big science test tomorrow," Wes answered. "I can't remember the names of the planets in order."

"I know a secret that will help you remember the order," said Keisha. "Remember this saying: My very energetic mother just sent us nine pizzas."

Wes looked surprised. "What do pizzas have to do with planets?" he asked.

Keisha smiled. "The first letter of each word is a clue to the name of the planet. My is the first word in the saying, so think about a planet name that begins with the letter m. It is the closest planet to the sun."

"Everyone knows Mercury is closest to the sun!" said Wes.

"Keep going," prompted Keisha. "Very is the second word in the saying. So think about a planet name that begins with the letter v."

"Venus!" shouted Wes. "I get it! That means the word energetic is a clue that the next planet is Earth."

"Now you get it," laughed Keisha.

"Thanks, Keisha! I'm going to do well on the test after all," said Wes.

The Science Test (cont.)

1. What is this story mainly about? _____
   _____

2. Name three objects that are in the solar system. _____
   _____

3. Why was Wes worried about the science test? _____
   _____

4. What saying helped Wes remember the order of the planet names?
   _____
   _____

5. Label the drawing with the names of the planets.

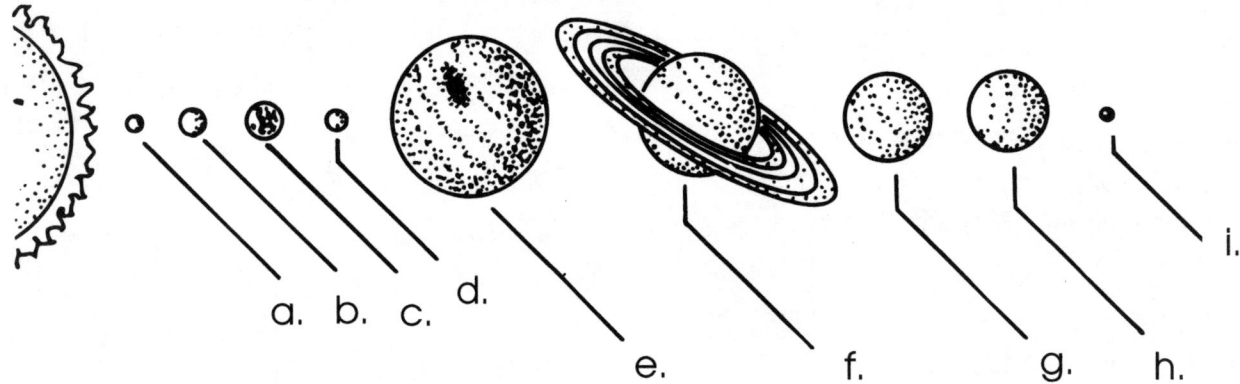

a. _____   f. _____
b. _____   g. _____
c. _____   h. _____
d. _____   i. _____
e. _____

Size Counts

All of the planets in the solar system are like spheres. They are round like balls. The chart below shows the diameter of each planet. The diameter is a line that passes through the center of a circle or sphere. The line goes from one side to the other. The longer the diameter, the bigger the planet.

Planet	Diameter in Miles	Diameter in Kilometers
Mercury	3,031	4,877
Venus	7,521	12,101
Earth	7,926	12,753
Mars	4,222	6,793
Jupiter	88,846	142,953
Saturn	74,898	120,511
Uranus	31,763	51,107
Neptune	30,800	49,577
Pluto	1,430	2,301

1. How is a planet like a sphere? _____

2. Which of the pictures shows a diameter? Circle it.

   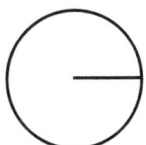   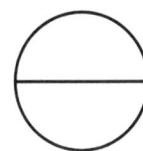

3. Which planet has about the same diameter as Earth? _____

4. Write the names of the planets in order from the smallest in size to the largest? _____

A Postcard from Rome

Dear Tia,

    We are staying in Rome now. It is a beautiful city. Today we went to the Trevi Fountain. It is a huge sculpture carved in marble. Water comes out of it. One of the shapes in the sculpture is Jupiter. He was an important god in a myth that people in Rome believed long ago. He was the king of all the gods. I remember our teacher telling us that the planet Jupiter was named for this god. It was the biggest planet, so it needed an important name.

    People say if you throw a coin into the fountain, you will come back to Rome someday. Of course, I had to throw a coin in. I hope I can come back and visit.

Love,
Kim

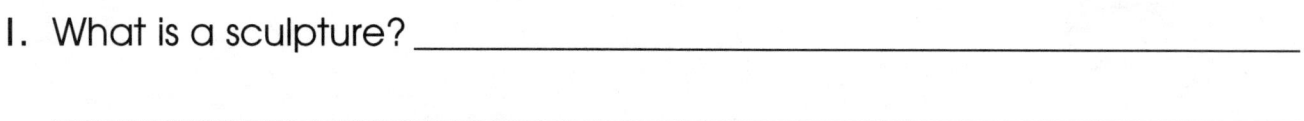

1. What is a sculpture? _____

2. Where is the Trevi Fountain? _____

3. Why was the biggest planet named Jupiter? _____

4. Which sentence in the postcard is an opinion? _____

On a Moonwalk

Tran and his little brother waited in line for their turn on the moonwalk. Tran watched the other children enter the bubble and bounce around. One girl leaped from one side of the moonwalk to the other in five jumps. Tran thought he could do it in four.

Tran's little brother tugged on his arm. "Why is this called a moonwalk?" he asked.

"There isn't much gravity on the moon," Tran said. "Gravity is what keeps things from flying into the air. Anyway, when the astronauts walked on the moon, it looked as though they were hopping."

"What did the astronauts do on the moon?" Tran's brother asked.

"First, the astronauts planted an American flag so everyone would know that an American had walked on the moon. Then they measured the air and looked inside some craters. They also picked up rocks and dirt to bring back to scientists on Earth."

"When I'm in the moonwalk, I'm going to pretend that I'm an astronaut," said Tran's brother. "I'm gong to look for moon rocks."

"Just don't plant a flag," said Tran. "You would let all the air out of the moonwalk."

1. How is walking in a moonwalk like walking on the moon?

   _____

   _____

2. While on the moon, why did the astronauts look as though they were

   hopping? _____

   _____

3. What did the astronauts do before picking up rocks and dirt?

   _____

4. Why do you think scientists wanted rocks and dirt from the moon?

   _____

   _____

Science   Name _____   Date _____

Going in Circles

Each morning the sun rises and moves across the sky. It lights our world and gives us heat. And each day the sun sets, bringing darkness. While it looks as though the sun travels across the sky, Earth is really the object that is moving.

Actually, Earth turns in two ways. Imagine a basketball spinning on your finger. Earth spins like the basketball. One time around is one rotation. It takes Earth 24 hours to spin around one time. One full rotation gives us one full day. We get night and day because of Earth's rotation.

While Earth rotates each day, it also moves a second way. To understand this kind of movement, imagine a tennis ball attached to a rope that someone swings overhead. The tennis ball follows the same path as it circles. Like the tennis ball, Earth follows a path as it circles, or orbits, around the sun. It takes 365 days for Earth to complete one orbit. One full orbit gives us one full year.

Now whenever you watch the sun rise and set and rise again, you will know that Earth has made one full rotation. And on each birthday, you will know that Earth has made one full orbit. How's that for going in circles?

1. The sun gives us heat and _____.

2. We get day and night because of Earth's _____.

3. It takes Earth 365 day to _____ around the sun.

4. Earth follows the same _____ as it moves around the sun.

Science   Name _____   Date _____

The North Star

A constellation is a group of stars that form a picture. For centuries, sailors used constellations to find their way across the sea. The constellations could tell them which way was north, south, east, or west.

The Big Dipper and the Little Dipper were two of the most important constellations for sailors. Each star group looked like a ladle. These two constellations helped sailors find the North Star. The sailors knew that when they looked at the North Star, they were facing north. Once they found north, the other directions were easy to find.

Here is how to find the North Star:
1. Find the Big Dipper in the night sky.
2. Find the two stars on the front of the bowl. These stars point to the Little Dipper.
3. Look for the handle on the Little Dipper.
4. Follow the stars to the end of the handle.

Do you see the brightest star on the end of the Little Dipper's handle? This star is the North Star.

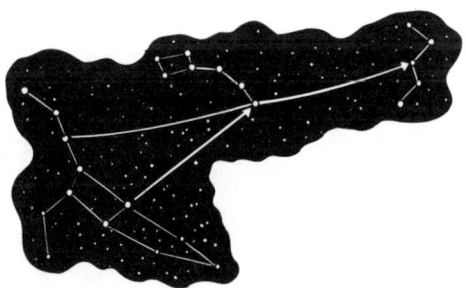

1. A constellation is ...
   a. a group of sailors.
   b. a group of stars.
   c. a group of cups.
   d. a group of pictures.

2. Where do you look after you find the Big Dipper?
   a. at the bowl of the Big Dipper
   b. at the bowl of the Little Dipper
   c. at the handle of the Little Dipper
   d. at the handle of the Big Dipper

3. Sailors used the Big Dipper and Little Dipper to ...
   a. drink water.
   b. put up sails.
   c. name stars.
   d. find north.

4. Suppose you are looking at the North Star. Which part of your body faces east?
   a. right arm
   b. left arm
   c. back
   d. nose

Social Studies   Name _____   Date_____

Out in Space

From about 1950 to 1990, the United States was in a war. It was called the Cold War. The other country in the war was the Soviet Union. The countries did not fight each other. Each country wanted to show it had the most power and the best leaders. One of the ways the countries competed was in space. Each country wanted to be the first one to learn about space. The people in both countries thought that winning the "space race" showed power.

The Cold War did not last. The United States and the Soviet Union, now called Russia, began to work together. They have joined with 14 other countries to build a large building in space. It is called a space station. The space station is bigger than four football fields. Astronauts live and work on the station for many months. They do experiments to learn about everything in the world. This project has not only helped us learn about our world but also helped the countries learn to work together.

1. Which country was in the Cold War?
   a. South Dakota
   b. South America
   c. Somalia
   d. The Soviet Union

2. In the Cold War, the countries wanted to show who had more
   a. people.
   b. power.
   c. astronauts.
   d. footballs.

3. The space station is a place ...
   a. to learn about the world.
   b. where countries fight.
   c. to play football.
   d. where people race.

4. The United States and Russia are now ...
   a. one country.
   b. friends.
   c. astronauts.
   d. fighting.

Math/Science   Name _____   Date_____

All in a Year

The sun is the center of the solar system. The nine planets orbit, or circle, around the sun. Each planet takes a different time to make one orbit. The time it takes to make one orbit is a year. The planets closer to the sun have shorter years than the planets that are farther away from the sun. The table below shows how long a year lasts on each planet.

Planet	Length of Planet's Year
Mercury	88 Earth days
Venus	225 Earth days
Earth	365 Earth days
Mars	687 Earth days
Jupiter	12 Earth years
Saturn	30 Earth years
Uranus	84 Earth years
Neptune	165 Earth years
Pluto	248 Earth years

1. Which planet has the shortest year? Which has the longest year? How do you know? _____

2. How many Earth days is Neptune's year? Show how you found the answer. _____

3. How many Earth days is Jupiter's year? Show how you found the answer. _____

4. Why did the author write this article? _____

I Want to Be a Knight

Dear Mother and Father,

I have finally settled in at Lord William's castle. I am excited about my job as his page. He has promised to teach me how to use small weapons. Lord William will also teach me how to behave as a knight. Part of the learning is that he must teach me numbers and studies of other worlds. You have already taught me to be brave and to care for the weak. So I think this part of being a page will be easy.

I have eight years here. Lord William says he will help me find a great knight to serve when I turn 15. I cannot wait to be a squire! It will be a hard job, but I will be one step closer to becoming a knight. As a squire, I must learn to set the table for my master and to serve his food. I must care for all of his armor, too. The best part of being a squire, though, is that I get to ride a horse, and I get trained as a knight. I can ride with my master wherever he goes.

If I do a good job, I hope to gain my sword and spurs of a knight by the time I am 20. I want to make you proud of me.

Your loving son,
Stephen

1. At what age does a boy begin his work as a page?
    a. 5
    b. 7
    c. 15
    d. 20

2. What happens after a boy completes his service as a page?
    a. He learns how knights behave.
    b. He becomes a knight.
    c. He goes to serve a knight.
    d. He becomes a squire.

3. Which of these is NOT a job of a squire?
    a. serve a knight dinner
    b. set a table for dinner
    c. learn math
    d. ride with a knight

4. What are two things a man gets when he becomes a knight?
    a. a sword and spurs
    b. a horse and spurs
    c. armor and a horse
    d. a horse and a sword

Tool Time

Directions: Read the story. Then answer the questions on page 36.

Farming was hard work in the Middle Ages. Poor peasants did all of the work. They had to raise crops for their families to eat, as well as for everyone in the castle. Most tools were cut out of wood. Very little iron was used at this time because people did not know how to melt iron. So how did the peasant farm? He had very simple tools, many of which we still use today.

A spade was a long tool with a point on one end. It was used for digging. Forks looked like spades, but they had three or four long fingers on the end. The fork was used for lifting hay and grass. Sickles were curved pieces of wood that peasants used to cut crops during harvest time. Scythes looked like sickles, except they had long handles. Scythes were swung from side to side to mow grass to make the hay.

To carry crops to the barn, peasants used stretchers. Stretchers were made using two poles with wood slats between the poles. It took two people to use a stretcher.

People in the Middle Ages found out how a plow worked. At first, the plow was not a helpful tool. The soil was hard for the plow to break through. But the horse harness was invented during the Middle Ages. It changed how the peasants farmed. Animals wore a harness, which made it easier for the animals to follow directions. Since oxen and horses were strong, they could pull the plow easily. People were able to make the plows heavier so they could cut through the soil. Farming became much easier.

Tool Time (cont.)

1. What were most tools made of?
   a. iron
   b. clay
   c. rock
   d. wood

2. What tool had long fingers on the end?
   a. a plow
   b. a fork
   c. a spade
   d. a scythe

3. What kind of movement did a sickle use?
   a. pushing
   b. chopping
   c. digging
   d. pulling

4. How was a sickle like a scythe?
   a. It had a long handle.
   b. It was used for digging.
   c. It was curved.
   d. It was made of iron.

5. What tool did the peasants use to mow?
   a. a spade
   b. a scythe
   c. a sickle
   d. a plow

6. What was one effect of the invention of the harness?
   a. Animals could pull heavier plows.
   b. It could dig deeper in the hard soil.
   c. It made animals stronger.
   d. It made soil easier to break.

7. Why did people need a heavier plow?
   a. Animals broke the plows because they were too light.
   b. Animals could not pull the plows because they were too light.
   c. Heavier plows cut through hard soil.
   d. Heavier plows cut through soft soil.

8. What tool do we use today that is like the spade?
   a. a shovel
   b. a rake
   c. an axe
   d. a saw

Social Studies   Name _____   Date _____

The Farming Life

May 1358

Dear Diary,

I met with Godwin and Erhland today. Godwin has three oxen, and Erhland has two oxen. I have three oxen and a plow. The three of us have made a schedule to use the plow and the animals to get the work done in the fields. We also have planned the days that each of us goes to the castle to get our work done for Lord Roger. We must work one or two days a week so he will continue to protect us.

We will take turns plowing, working at the castle, shearing the sheep, and repairing our homes. It works out well that we share our animals and tools. It takes eight oxen to get one acre plowed each day. We are able to get our work done and meet our responsibilities to our lord.

Galord

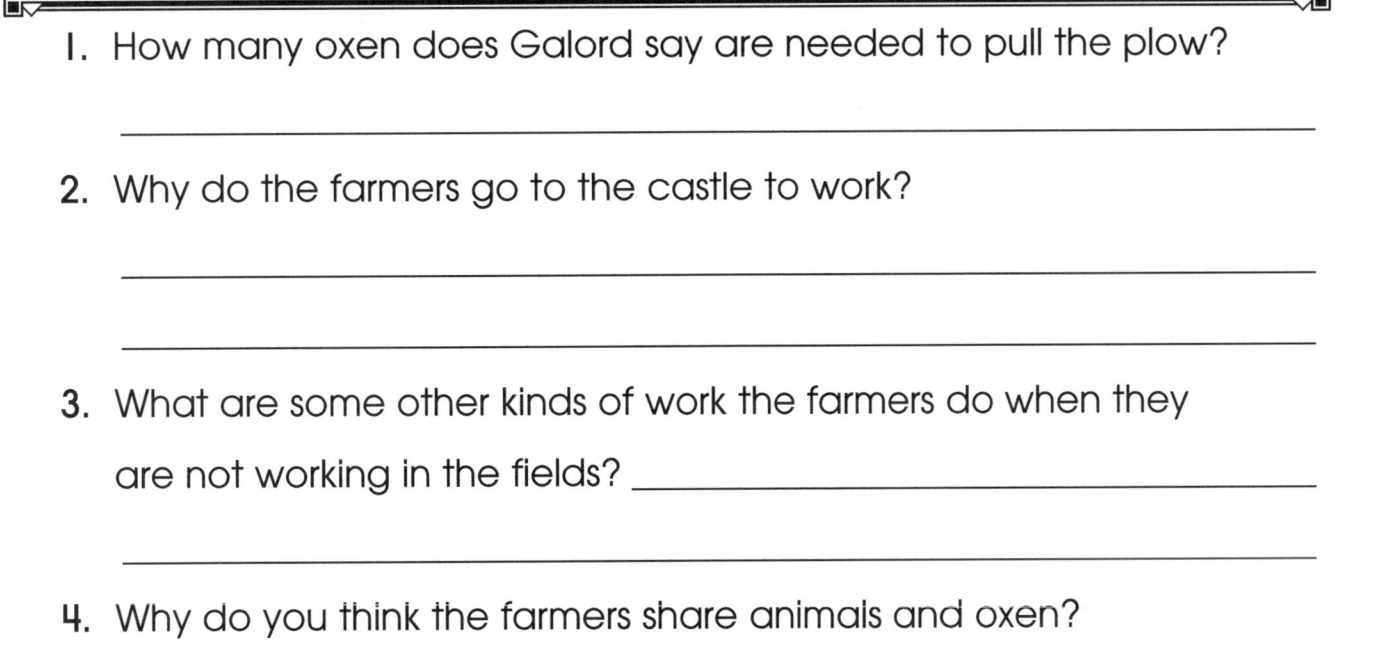

1. How many oxen does Galord say are needed to pull the plow?

2. Why do the farmers go to the castle to work?

3. What are some other kinds of work the farmers do when they are not working in the fields?

4. Why do you think the farmers share animals and oxen?

Social Studies   Name _____   Date _____

Castles

A castle was the place a king or a lord lived during the Middle Ages. But a castle was more than a home. It was like a small city.

A castle had a place for knights and soldiers to stay. These people were very important because they helped keep the castle safe when other people attacked. Some of the soldiers worked in the armory. The armory was the place where craftsmen made armor and swords.

The castle had places to store food. Women salted meat so it would not spoil. The meat was stored in cool places. Grain and fruit were stored in special rooms, too. The people in the castle needed enough food to feed everyone in the castle for a whole year.

The castle had a treasure room that held all of the money, jewels, and gold the lord owned. Some soldiers had to guard this room to keep the treasures safe.

A castle also had one large room called a great hall. During the day, everyone ate and talked there. This was usually the only room that had a fire.

People who lived and farmed on the lord's land would come to the great hall, too. They wanted to meet with the lord if they thought they were not being treated fairly. The lord was the ruler of the castle and the land around it. He made the rules. So the great room was also a place of government. At night, the great hall became a huge bedroom.

A castle was more than just a home for the lord, it was a safe place for the whole community.

1. A castle was like a _____.

2. A bank today could be compared to the _____ room in a castle.

3. A mayor today could be compared to the _____ of the castle because he made the rules.

4. The rooms that kept the food could be compared to _____ stores today.

Arts   Name _____   Date _____

Catherine Helps

Catherine looked at her father. He quickly pulled the thread through the shuttle. He tied the thread to the piece of wood. The shuttle was the part of the loom that moved through the base threads. The shuttle pulled the thread that made the colorful design in the cloth. Catherine's father was known for weaving the best wool cloth in the town. Catherine was proud that she could help her family in their business.

Catherine helped her father shear the sheep of their wool. Then Catherine and her mother washed the fleece. It was Catherine's job to comb the fleece. Combing removed the tangles and dirt. Catherine was very careful to make the fleece smooth.

Next, Catherine's mother spun the fleece into yarn. She put some of the fleece on a stick called a distaff. Catherine's mother spun the distaff and let the yarn fall to the ground. The big ball of fluff became a long thread of yarn. Catherine loved to roll the yarn into a big ball.

Finally, the wool was dyed into beautiful colors. Everyone in the family helped with the dying. But now it was her father's turn. The weaving was the last step. This step took the most time. But the cloth was beautiful. It always sold for a good price.

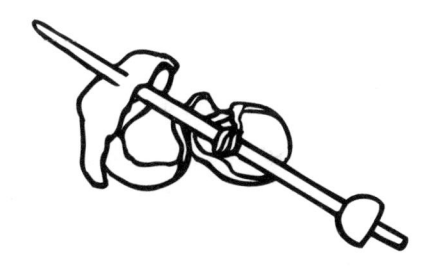

1. What tool is used to weave? _____

2. Why did Catherine comb the fleece?
   _____
   _____

3. What happened before the yarn was dyed?
   _____
   _____

4. What kind of cloth was made from the fleece of sheep?
   _____

A Farming Experiment

During the Middle Ages, the peasant farmers found out that their crops were not as rich and healthy as they had been in the past. For years, they had divided their fields into two parts. One part was planted in the spring. The other part was planted in the fall. The soil in each part was planted every year. The farmers thought the soil needed to rest so the crops would be healthier.

The farmers tried something new. They went to a three-field rotation system. They divided their fields into three parts. One part was planted in the spring, and one part was planted in the fall. The last field was left to rest for a whole year. The next year the farmers would grow crops on the unplanted field and only one of the fields used the previous year. After three years, each of the parts had a chance to rest. After several years, the farmers found that their crops were more healthy and abundant. They also found that they could grow more crops with their new farming system.

1. Why did the farmers think the soil needed to rest?

   _____

   _____

2. How often did the farmers plant the crops that did not grow well?

   _____

3. How did the farmers experiment with farming?

   _____

   _____

4. What was the three-field rotation system?

   _____

   _____

Arts

What Fun!

Long ago most people could not read or write. They did not own computers or televisions. They did not even have soccer balls or baseballs or other fun games to play. So what did people do for fun a long time ago? They watched minstrels perform!

A minstrel was a person who could do many things. A minstrel was an actor and a storyteller. The person also sang, danced, and played musical instruments. Some minstrels could even juggle balls!

Often a group of minstrels traveled together. They gave shows in return for food and a place to stay. The group would stay in one place for several days. Then they would move to a new town. Some wealthy kings and lords hired a minstrel to live with them. Then there was fun and laughter each night. No one needed television when there was a minstrel in the castle!

1. Write a summary of this article. _____
_____
_____

2. How did minstrels get paid? _____
_____

3. Why do you think minstrels traveled to different places?
_____
_____

4. How is a minstrel like an actor we see on television today?
_____

This Is an Acre

An acre is used to measure land. This measurement was invented during the Middle Ages. In that time, peasants were given land to farm. It was not really their land, but they had to grow crops on it. They could keep most of the crops, but part of the goods went to the lord who owned the land.

The lord divided the land into acres. He decided who would get the land. Some peasants got one acre. Others got several acres. The lord gave out the land based on the number of people in each family.

An acre of land was always shaped like a rectangle. It measured 220 feet (67 m) long and 22 feet (7 m) wide. So how were these measurements decided? They were based on the use of the plow!

Eight oxen pulled a plow. The peasant and oxen had to plow one acre each day. The oxen could pull the plow 220 feet (67 m) before they had to rest. The length of an acre was chosen by how long the oxen could work before resting.

The width of an acre was determined by a tool the peasants used. The peasants used a rod to make the oxen move. The rod was five and one-half yards long. The acre measurement was set to be four times the rod length—22 feet (7 m). So the amount a peasant had to plow each day was 220 feet (67 m) long by 22 feet (7 m) wide—one acre.

1. What was the shape of a field in the Middle Ages?

   _____

2. What was the perimeter of these fields? _____
   Draw a picture on the back of this paper and label the length of each side.

3. How did the people decide what an acre would be?

   _____

   _____

4. Do you think this was a good way to measure land? Why or why not?

   _____

   _____

Social Studies

Marco Polo Returns

Directions: Read the story. Then answer the questions on page 44.

After 24 years of exploring, Marco Polo finally returned home.

"I never thought I would see him again," said Aldo, a long-time friend.

Marco, his father, and his uncle left Italy when Marco was 17. Since that time, Marco had traveled all over Asia. The Polos spent most of those years in China. They were the guests of the ruler of that large country. The ruler in China was the Khan.

"I could speak four languages," said Marco. "The Khan sent me to talk to people in his kingdom. The Khan gave me many treasures for pay!"

After a while, the Polos began to worry about their safety. The Khan was very old. They thought he might die soon. They thought a fight might break out in China. The Polos decided it was time to go home.

Marco said, "The Khan liked us and did not want us to leave. We had to sneak out of China."

Once home, the Polos talked about many interesting things they had seen. The people used black stones to heat their houses. Also, their money was made out of paper, not metal. It had pictures of the Khan on it. Marco talked of a machine that printed the pictures on the money.

It seemed the Khan also set up a delivery system. He could send messages to people who lived far away. There were places in which people, or messengers, lived all over the country. One messenger would ride on a horse until he got to one of these places. Then another messenger would ride to the next place. This system did not work the horses as hard, and the message was delivered more quickly.

"It feels so good to be home!" exclaimed Marco. "But I like to travel. I hope to go to other places someday."

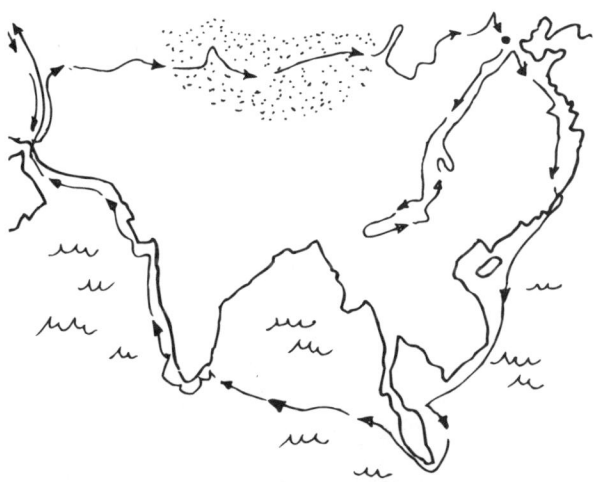

Social Studies   Name _____   Date_____

Marco Polo Returns (cont.)

1. How long had Marco been gone?
   _____

2. How did knowing so many languages help Marco in China?
   _____
   _____

3. Why did Marco sneak out of China?
   _____
   _____

4. How was the money in China different from that in Italy?
   _____
   _____

5. People in the Middle Ages made books by writing each page by hand. Why would a machine that printed pictures interest them?
   _____
   _____

6. How is the postal system we have today like the one used in China?
   _____
   _____
   _____
   _____

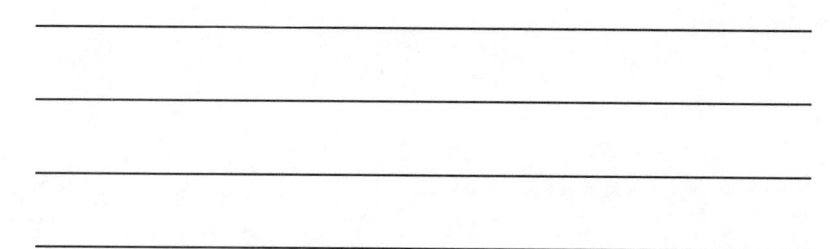

Social Studies   Name _____   Date _____

Join a Guild

The Middle Ages was a time when people traveled to new places. The people brought back new foods, new cloth, and new inventions. The people who brought back the goods and sold them were called merchants.

Traveling took a lot of time. It was dangerous work, too. The trip was long, and losing the goods was easy. The merchants decided to join together to form guilds, or groups. People who sold the same kinds of goods joined one guild. People in a guild could buy larger amounts of goods more cheaply. They also set a price at which the goods could be sold and the pay the workers would get. If a merchant was not in a guild, he or she could not sell the item. People from other countries who brought new goods to sell were not allowed to sell in the market. There was a chance a new person might sell the same goods at a cheaper price. So the guild made rules that said only a person in a guild could sell certain goods.

Many guilds became powerful and tried to make rules in the town. They also collected money to help pay for important needs.

1. What did a merchant do?

_____

_____

2. What do you think the word *goods* means?

_____

_____

3. Who could join a guild? _____

_____

4. What might happen if a person outside of a guild sold his or her goods at a price cheaper than the one set by the guild?

_____

Social Studies   Name _____   Date _____

Children Help, Too

Dear Daniel,	Dear Millie,
Here are the chores you are to do today.	Here are the chores you are to do today.
1. Collect a full day's supply of buffalo chips to keep a fire going in the cook stove.	1. Milk the cow in the morning.
2. Harness the horses to the plow.	2. Gather the hen's eggs.
3. Help your dad plow the north field in the morning.	3. Keep the fire going in the cook stove in the morning.
4. Keep the fire in the cook stove going in the afternoon.	4. Watch your baby sister while I prepare the noontime meal.
5. Write your facts to ten in the dirt.	5. Cook a johnnycake.
6. Milk the cow at night.	6. Mend Dad's torn shirt sleeve.
7. Help your dad feed the animals at night.	7. Write your alphabet in the dirt three times.
You and your sister may play after supper.	8. Help me wash and stack the supper dishes.
	You and your brother may play after dinner.

1. Who do you think is older, the brother or the sister?

   Tell why you think so. _____
   _____

2. What chores did both children have in common?
   _____

3. What chores did girls have to do? What chores did boys have to do?
   _____
   _____
   _____

© McGraw-Hill Children's Publishing   46   0-7424-1923-1 Theme-Based Reading Comprehension

Science   Name _____   Date _____

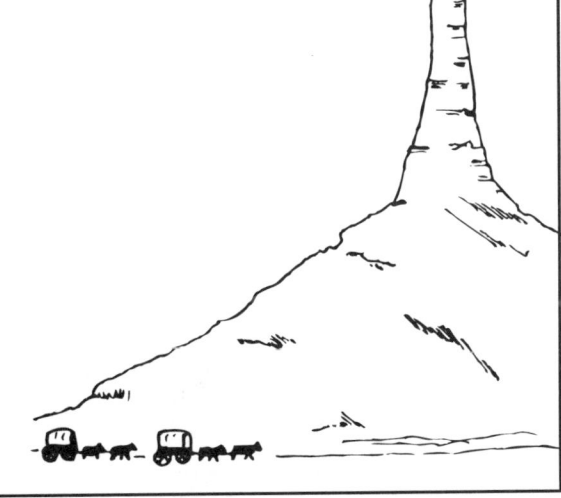

Landforms on the Oregon Trail

Directions: Read the diary entry. Then answer the questions on page 48.

Dear Diary,

   It has been a long trip, and we are only half way done. We left Independence, Missouri, in May. Father, Mother, Agnes, and I started to drive our wagon on the Oregon Trail with 30 other families. The trail is said to be 2,000 miles (3,218 km) long. The first part of the trail was not too difficult. The weather and land were pleasant. There were many forests to keep us cool, and there was lots of water. We were able to hunt for food to save our supplies for the hard part of the trip that was to come.

   At Fort Kearney, we began to follow a river. The land we crossed was called the plains. It is a good name. The land is flat and dry. Luckily, there was lots of water when we followed the river. But there were few trees. There were times when we barely had enough wood to cook our food. Sometimes it looked as though we were riding in a sea of grass. The days were hot and the nights were cold.

   After three months on the trail, we are wondering if we will ever make it to California. We hear the hardest part of the trip is to come. We must cross the Rocky Mountains. There is one pass we must take the wagon through. We must do it before the winter snow comes and closes the road. It is already getting very cold. Once we get through the mountains, we must cross a great desert. The plains do not look so bad when I think about the desert. It will be even hotter. Water will be even harder to find.

   The thought of forests and land in California drives us on.
I know we will make it.
Matthew

Landforms on the Oregon Trail (cont.)

1. How long was the Oregon Trail?
   a. 100 miles (161 km)
   b. 200 miles (322 km)
   c. 1,000 miles (1,609 km)
   d. 2,000 miles (3,218 km)

2. In which month did Matthew write this diary entry?
   a. June
   b. July
   c. November
   d. May

3. Where did the pioneers go after leaving Independence, Missouri?
   a. Fort Kearney
   b. California
   c. the desert
   d. the plains

4. The plains were ...
   a. wet and cold.
   b. high and rocky.
   c. flat and grassy.
   d. hot and dry.

5. Why was it difficult to start a fire on the plains?
   a. The grass would burn and start a big fire.
   b. There was little wood.
   c. It rained all the time
   d. The family ran out of matches.

6. What would happen if the pioneers did not cross the mountains before the snow fell?
   a. They would not get through the pass.
   b. They would need to build a sled.
   c. They would need to return to Fort Kearney.
   d. They would need to find a cave to live in for the winter.

7. What kind of land would the pioneers travel on after the mountains?
   a. a forest
   b. a valley
   c. a plain
   d. a desert

Social Studies/Math Name _____ Date_____

You're Invited to a House-Raising

Dear Neighbors,

The Jackson family moved to the area last year. They have been living in a lean-to since then. It has been hard on the family and will not keep them safe during the coming fall and winter months. They will need a log cabin very soon.

Mr. Jackson has worked hard to fell trees this spring. Like the rest of us, he does not have nails to keep the logs in place. So, he has cut the ends of the logs so they will fit together on the corners.

Mr. Jackson is now ready to build the log cabin. He is asking us to join him for a house-raising next month. This log cabin will be like most. It will be 20 feet (6 m) long and 16 feet (5 m) wide. It will be 7 feet (2 m) high.

Once the logs are in place, the women and children can do the chinking. They will add the mud, clay, and moss between the logs. It's important that the wind and cold not get inside. The Jackson children could easily become sick.

It should not take much longer to do the roof. A few logs across the top and some cut boards to cover them are all that is needed. Once the cabin is done, there will be a big celebration with lots of food, singing, and dancing. I'm sure we will see you there.

Your neighbor,
Ben Tyler

Math   Name _____   Date _____

You're Invited to a House-Raising (cont.)

1. What season do you think it is? How do you know?

   _____

   _____

2. Why do you think pioneers lived in lean-tos when they first found land?

   _____

   _____

3. Why do you think women and children did the chinking?

   _____

   _____

4. Draw a picture of the finished cabin. Make sure you show how long, wide, and tall it is.

5. Why do you think the people celebrated when the cabin was done?

   _____

   _____

6. Why do you think it was important for the neighbors to help the Jackson family? _____

   _____

Math   Name _____   Date _____

Johnnycakes

JOHNNYCAKES
Makes 1 9-inch johnnycake
- 1 cup (237 ml) corn meal
- 1 cup (237 ml) flour
- $\frac{3}{4}$ cup (177 ml) brown sugar
- $\frac{1}{4}$ tablespoon (7 ml) salt
- 1 tablespoon (15 ml) baking soda
- 1 beaten egg
- 1 cup (237 ml) buttermilk
- $\frac{1}{4}$ cup (59 ml) shortening

1. Grease an iron skillet.
2. Mix all ingredients together.
3. Pour the batter in the skillet, and cover with a lid.
4. Place the skillet on top of hot coals and cover the lid with coals.
5. Cook for 20 minutes.

1. How much corn meal would be needed if someone made ten johnnycakes?
   a. 1 cup
   b. 4 cups
   c. 5 cups
   d. 10 cups

2. What happens after the skillet is put in the hot coals?
   a. The ingredients are mixed together.
   b. The johnnycake is ready to eat.
   c. The batter cooks for 20 minutes.
   d. The skillet gets washed.

3. How many cups of ingredients are needed?
   a. 1 cup
   b. 4 cups
   c. 5 cups
   d. 10 cups

4. How many tablespoons of ingredients are needed?
   a. 1 tablespoon
   b. $1\frac{1}{2}$ tablespoons
   c. 2 tablespoons
   d. $2\frac{1}{2}$ tablespoons

Math   Name _____   Date _____

Packing for the Trip

Read the following packing list for a pioneer wagon train. Answer the questions.

Food	Amount	Cost
Bacon	600 lb. (272 kg)	$30.00
Baking soda	10 lb. (4.5 kg)	$1.00
Coffee	100 lb. (45 kg)	$8.00
Flour, five barrels	1,080 lb. (490 kg)	$20.00
Fruit, dried	50 lb. (23 kg)	$3.00
Rice	75 lb. (34 kg)	$3.75
Salt, pepper, and other herbs	10 lb. (4.5 kg)	$1.00
Sugar	150 lb. (68 kg)	$7.00
Tea	5 lb. (2 kg)	$2.75

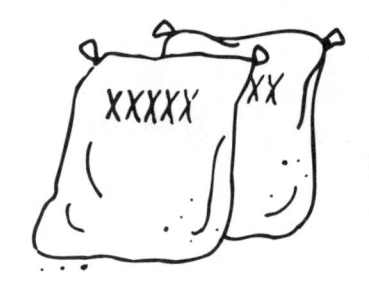

1. If travelers followed this list, how many pounds of food would they carry? Show your work.

2. How much money would people spend on food? Show your work.

3. One pound of rice today costs about $1.00. If pioneers had to buy rice today, how much would they pay? Show your work.

Arts   Name   Date

Kitchen Music

Settlers had to work hard to build a farm. Everyone in the family had to help. But families made time for fun, especially music. Some settlers did have pianos and fiddles, but most of the people had to find other ways to make music. They did not have to look too far, though. Several instruments were right in their kitchens.

Spoons were used as one kind of instrument. The backs of two spoons were held together in one hand. A player hit the spoons between a leg and the other hand to make a clacking sound.

Another instrument that settlers played was a clay jug. A sound was made by blowing air from the mouth across the jug's opening. Different-sized jugs made different sounds. Big jugs made lower tones. Small jugs made higher tones.

Another popular instrument was a washboard. A washboard was made of metal and wood. The metal part had ridges. When stroked with the hand or a spoon, it made a sound like a zip.

1. Settlers used from things their _____ to make instruments.

2. Two _____ placed back to back made a clacking sound.

3. They blew air across the opening of a _____.

4. A _____ made a zip sound.

Social Studies   Name _____   Date _____

Problems on the Plains

At one time, huge herds of buffalo lived on the plains. The Native Americans followed the buffalo. These people needed the animals to live. The animals were used for meat. The hides were used for clothing. The bones were used for tools and jewelry. The tendons were used to string bows.

The plains began to change. Settlers began farming the land. A railroad soon followed. It was built from one side of the country to the other. Many buffalo were killed to help feed the railroad workers. Other buffalo were killed for their hides. The number of buffalo dropped to only 100,000.

The United States government did not stop the killing. They hoped that the Native Americans would move to reservations if the buffalo were gone. A reservation was land on which the tribes would live. The government promised food, buildings, tools, and schools. Some people did move to the reservations. But the government did not keep their promises. The Native Americans became hungry. Many returned to the plains to look for food.

The Native Americans found that their land had changed. They became angry. Some attacked the settlers living there. American soldiers were sent west to get the Native Americans to move back to the reservation. They would not go back. The two groups began fighting. The Native Americans did not have the weapons to fight the trained soldiers, and they lost the fight. They were sent back to the reservations.

1. What two changes happened on the plains to make the Native Americans angry? _____

_____

2. Why were so many buffalo killed? _____

_____

3. Why might the government have wanted the Native Americans moved off the plains? _____

_____

© McGraw-Hill Children's Publishing   0-7424-1923-1 Theme-Based Reading Comprehension

Science   Name _____   Date _____

Life in a Desert

Directions: Read the story. Then answer the questions on page 56.

Tran looked out the window. He and his mother were driving through the Great Basin, a large area of deserts in the United States. He could see rocks shaped like arches and tables. They seemed to grow from the flat, sandy land. Tran could also see heat rise up from the road.

"It has to be at least 120 degrees out there," Tran said out loud.

"I don't think it's quite that hot," answered his mother. "But the temperature in this desert can get up to 100°F (38°C) during the day. That's why you don't see too many animals right now. They hide in their burrows where it's cool during the day. They come out to look for food at night when it is cooler. Desert temperatures drop to around 75°F (24°C) at night."

"How can animals even live out there?" Tran asked. "There's no water."

"It's true that a desert is dry," agreed Mrs. Akira. "Only about ten inches of rain falls in the Great Basin. The animals have learned to live with little water, though. They have adapted to life in a desert."

"How can anything live without water?" said Tran.

"Most of the animals are very small, like the kangaroo rat," said Mrs. Akira. "It eats seeds that it finds. The seeds have small amounts of water in them. Other animals eat cactus plants. Cactuses can store lots of water inside. One animal, the desert turtle, can go a whole year without drinking any water."

"Well, I can't imagine going one hour without water in the desert," said Tran. "I don't see how the pioneers crossed this desert. I am certainly glad we have a car with air conditioning."

Science   Name _____   Date _____

Life in a Desert (cont.)

1. What is the name of the desert area in the United States?

   a. the Great Basin
   b. the Great Desert
   c. the Desert Turtle
   d. the Arch Desert

2. What is the difference in the day and night temperatures of the desert in the story?

   a. 20°
   b. 100°
   c. 25°
   d. 45°

3. What does *adapted* mean in this story?

   a. a place to live
   b. learned to live with
   c. no water
   d. hot temperatures

4. Which animal can live a year without water?

   a. a desert turtle
   b. a kangaroo rat
   c. a rattlesnake
   d. an elf owl

5. How do most desert animals get water?

   a. They drink from rivers.
   b. They drink from rocks.
   c. They get it from sand.
   d. They get it from food.

6. Why are many desert animals more active at night?

   _____
   _____

Social Studies   Name _____   Date_____

Pioneer Troubles

Directions: Read the article. Then answer the questions on page 58.

Pioneers moved west hoping for a better life. They knew that the land was free if they worked on it for five years. The trip was gong to be hard. Building a farm would be even harder. These families, called homesteaders, found out exactly how hard farming on the plains would be.

The settlers lived in fear that Native Americans would harm them. The Native Americans were angry that strangers were living on their land. Each year, more and more land was being taken from the Native Americans.

The plains were flat and grassy. There were few trees with which to build homes, to make fences, or to use for firewood. Settlers learned to use what the land had to offer. Homes were made out of sod, or cut grass. They would make a frame of trees they could find. Then they covered it with squares of grass they cut from the ground. To make fires, settlers used the dried droppings of cows and buffaloes. Settlers kept only the animals they needed to work the farm or to provide food.

Several inventions helped the settlers live on the plains. The most important invention was barbed wire. Farmers could keep animals in one place. The barbed wire allowed settlers to keep herds of cattle. They could earn money with the cattle and also use them for food. The windmill was another invention that changed life on the plains. Farmers did not have to wait on the rain to water dry crops in the summer. They used windmills to pump water out of the ground. This made keeping their crops healthy much easier.

Pioneer life was hard, but they made it better by adapting and solving problems creatively.

Social Studies   Name _____   Date_____

Pioneer Troubles (cont.)

1. How did homesteaders get free land?
   _____
   _____

2. What does the word *homesteader* mean? If you don't know, look it up and write a definition in your own words.
   _____
   _____

3. Why was the lack of trees a problem for settlers on the plains?
   _____
   _____

4. How did barbed wire change the life of settlers living on the plains?
   _____
   _____

5. How did the windmill change the life of settlers living on the plains?
   _____
   _____

Arts

A Cloth Picture

Directions: Read the article. Then answer the questions on page 60.

A quilt is made with two large pieces of cloth sewed together. Stuffing is placed between the cloth and it is sewn to keep it all together. Colorful patches of cloth are sewed into the top to make a pattern. Most people think of a quilt as a blanket—something that keeps someone warm. But in the pioneer days, quilts did more than keep people warm. They had many other purposes.

On a trip west, dishes were packed in quilts to keep them from breaking. They also covered hard wagon seats on bumpy roads. During a dust storm, quilts were stuffed in the holes of wagons to keep out dirt. Once pioneers were living in a cabin, the quilts covered windows to keep out the cold and rain. But they had other uses, too. They brightened up a dark room as they lay on a bed or hung on a wall. They became pictures in cloth.

Quilts quickly became a kind of art to pioneer women. Quilters wanted to make something that was pretty to look at. They thought about the colors that would go together. They thought about the pattern they would make. Some quilters wanted to tell a story. So, they sewed patterns that told about an important event their lives.

The log cabin pattern was very popular with pioneer women. It had a red square in the middle. The red square was a symbol of the fire in a cabin. Light and dark fabric strips were sewed around the square. A woman might choose this pattern once she had lived in a log cabin. Other patterns were named "barn raising" and "courthouse steps."

Pioneer women looked forward to the making quilts. They would invite all of their neighbors to a quilting bee. Women did not get to see friends too often, so a quilting bee was a time for women to work and talk at the same time. The women would work together to make one quilt. Often a quilt was completed in one day.

Many of these quilts that were so lovingly made are passed from family member to family member to remind them of their family's past.

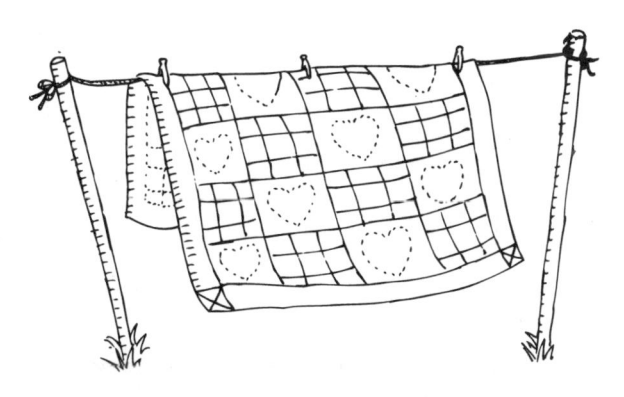

Art　　　　　Name _____　　　　　Date_____

A Cloth Picture (cont.)

1. Name two ways that a quilt is art.

   _____
   _____

2. Name three ways that pioneers used a quilt.

   _____
   _____
   _____
   _____

3. List one other creative use for a quilt.

   _____

4. Why might a pioneer woman choose a to make a quilt with a pattern called "barn raising"?

   _____
   _____

5. Why did pioneer women look forward to a quilting bee?

   _____
   _____

6. Make up one other kind of pattern for a quilt. Think about an important event, person, or time of year. What would be a good quilt pattern?

   _____

Why Animals Can't Talk

Directions: Read the story. Then answer the questions on page 62.

In the beginning, animals could talk. They lived on the land by themselves. Then the Iroquois people came. The animals were excited about the visitors, and they showed the people how to live on the land so that they would stay. Wolf took them to the best places to hunt. Beaver made large dams so the people would have water and fish. Sheep took them to the greenest fields to find safe plants to eat. Dog stayed with the people to help them hunt. Dog liked the people so much that he even watched over their children.

Life was good for the Iroquois, and the people grew in number. They soon lived all across the land. After awhile, it was harder for Wolf and Beaver to find food. Sheep was feeling crowded. Some of the animals were angry. They called a meeting to decide how to solve the problem.

"I think we should eat all the people to make them go away," said Wolf.

"That is too cruel," said Beaver. "Let's just knock their houses down and chase them away."

"There is no need to harm them," said Sheep. "Why don't we just lead them to new land?" asked Sheep.

"I like the people," said Dog. "We should learn to share."

All of the sudden, the Great Spirit appeared. "You animals should feel ashamed!" he said. "Because you want to harm the people, I will take away something from you. From now on, no animal will ever talk again."

The animals stood in silence. Dog spoke first, "Please, Great Spirit, not all of us wanted to harm the people."

"Should all of us be punished the same?" asked sheep.

The Great Spirit thought for a minute. Then he answered, "True, not all of you wanted to harm the people, but all of you are here at this meeting. So, the animals will still lose your gift of speech. However, the punishment will be different for each."

The Great Spirit looked at Wolf. "You wanted to kill the people, so now the people will want to kill you," he said. "You will be the enemy of the people."

Then the Great Spirit turned to Beaver. "You only wanted to knock down the people's houses and chase them away," said the Great Spirit. "They will do the same to you. They will think you are a problem and chase you out of the lakes."

"Sheep, you only wanted to lead the people away," the Great Spirit said. "Since you did not want to harm the people, they will not harm you. From now, on you will go where they lead you."

(continued on page 62)

Language Arts/Social Studies   Name_____   Date_____

Why Animals Can't Talk (cont.)

Finally, the Great Spirit looked at Dog. "Dog, you wanted to share with the people, so they will share with you. You will continue to live with the people. While you cannot talk, you will understand their words."

And that is why animals can't talk.

1. Do the people trust Dog? Tell why you think so.
   _____
   _____

2. Why was it harder for Wolf and Beaver to find food?
   _____
   _____

3. What happens after the Great Spirit arrives?
   _____

4. Do you think it was fair that the Great Spirit took away the gift of speech from all the animals? Explain._____
   _____
   _____

Pookie's Walk

Directions: Read the story. Then answer the questions on page 64.

"Come on, Pookie, it's time for our walk," called Zoe.

Pookie raced to the door. Her fluffy tail wagged from side to side as she waited patiently for Zoe to fasten the leash on her collar. As soon as Zoe opened the door, the little Cocker spaniel bolted down the steps, dragging Zoe with her.

"Slow down, Pookie," laughed Zoe. "I promise we'll walk around the whole neighborhood today."

Zoe and Pookie headed north on Lake Road. They walked for one block and then turned left on Main Street. Pookie saw several dogs at the park and barked loudly.

"If you stop and bark, we won't be able to do the whole loop," said Zoe. Pookie gave one final bark and took the lead once again. The two walked west for three blocks.

Zoe saw her friend Tom on Mountain View Road and waved.

"I'm heading to the library," Tom said.

Zoe and Pookie quickly walked three blocks south and turned left at the ball fields. Pookie continued to charge ahead on Maple Street.

Pookie was on autopilot. She knew the way home from the library. Pookie went to the end of the block and turned left on Lake Road. All of the sudden, Pookie stopped, sat down, and looked at Zoe.

"Are you ready to race?" asked Zoe. "You usually beat me, but I think I have a chance to win today."

Zoe unfastened the leash and watched the dog sprint forward. Zoe ran as fast as she could, but she could not catch the speeding dog running the last block home. By the time Zoe got back to the house, Pookie lay calmly on the porch steps.

"Next time, Pookie, I get a head start!" panted Zoe.

Math   Name _____   Date _____

Pookie's Walk (cont.)

1. What is the story mainly about?
   a. a girl who takes her dog to the park
   b. a girl who takes her dog on a neighborhood walk
   c. a girl who walks to the library
   d. a girl who likes to race her dog

2. Zoe lives on ...
   a. Maple Street.
   b. Main Street.
   c. Oak Street.
   d. Lake Road.

3. On Main Street, Zoe and Pookie walked ...
   a. for three blocks.
   b. to the library.
   c. to the park.
   d. to see Tom.

4. How many blocks did Zoe and Pookie walk?
   a. 4
   b. 7
   c. 9
   d. 13

5. Draw a map showing where Zoe and Pookie walked.

Science   Name _____   Date _____

Caring for Speckles

Dear Basha,

Thank you for taking care of Speckles while I'm gone. Here is a list of what you need to do for her.

1. Speckles needs to be fed twice each day. Her food is in the cabinet under the sink. Just open a food packet and pour it in her bowl. She may not eat right away because she prefers to eat when no one is watching. The food should be gone the next time you visit.

2. Speckles needs fresh water twice each day. Just change her water at the same time you feed her. Sometime Speckles uses her paw to splash in her water dish. Please clean up any water that gets on the floor because Speckles will track wet footprints through the house.

3. Speckles needs lots of exercise. Even though Speckles is an indoor pet, she still needs to run and play. If you toss her toy mouse or ball of yarn, she will chase it. It's funny the way Speckles sneaks up and pounces on her toys.

4. Speckles needs to be groomed. She sheds lots of hair, so she needs to be brushed once each day to get rid of the loose hair. Her brush is under the sink next to her food.

5. Speckles needs lots of love! She will be lonely since I'm not home with her. Hold her and pet her when you visit. She will purr very loudly for you.

Thank you for taking care of my precious pet.

Your friend,

Lily

1. What kind of pet is Speckles?
   a. a dog
   b. a frog
   c. a cat
   d. a mouse

2. Which is NOT a kind of care that Speckles needs?
   a. food
   a. love
   c. water
   d. walking

3. What does *shed* mean?
   a. to lose
   b. to clean
   c. to eat
   d. to brush

4. What makes Speckles purr?
   a. feeding her
   b. petting her
   c. washing her
   d. chasing her

Science Name _____ Date_____

Aquarium Competition

Jake opened the lid of his aquarium. Most of the fish quickly swam to the top. They knew it was time for dinner. Jake paused before sprinkling the food across the water. He noticed that one little fish stayed away from the others. Its fins were looking ragged. Jake wondered whether the fish might be sick.

Jake tapped the can, and the food fell out. He saw one big fish rush to the top and gobble most of the food. This same fish nipped at the fins of the smaller fish whenever it tried to grab a bite.

"I see why the fins are ragged," thought Jake. "That little fish isn't sick at all. The bigger fish is just picking on it."

Jake got out a smaller fish bowl. He poured some tank water into the bowl, scooped the ragged fish out of the aquarium with a net, and gently put it in the small bowl.

"There you go, little guy!" said Jake. "I'll give you lots of food and some time to grow. When you get big and strong, I'll put you back in the aquarium again. Then you will be able to compete with that bully fish!"

1. In this story, what does *compete* mean?
   a. to get to the top of the tank faster
   b. to be a bigger bully
   c. to grow bigger than others
   d. to swim faster than others

2. The bigger fish nipped the fins of the smaller fish because it wanted to ...
   a. eat the fins of the smaller fish.
   b. keep the smaller fish away from the food.
   c. show the fish friendship.
   d. show the smaller fish how strong it was.

3. What will probably happen to the smaller fish?
   a. It will stay the same because fish don't grow.
   b. It will grow because it will get more to eat.
   c. It will grow because it will have more room to swim.
   d. It will die.

4. What does it mean to be a bully?

   _____
   _____
   _____

Math   Name _____   Date _____

Small, Medium, and Large Dogs

Are you thinking about getting a new dog?
At Perfect Pet, we have big dogs,
medium dogs, and small dogs!

Mastiff
Weight: up to 185 pounds (84 kg)
Lots of exercise.
Large yard to run

Labrador Retriever
Weight: up to 75 pounds (34 kg)
Working dogs, need exercise
Like to play and jump

Pekingese
Weight: up to 10 pounds (4.5 kg)
Small, lap dog

1. What is the largest dog and how much does it weigh?
   _____

2. What is the weight difference in the sizes of the medium and small dog?
   _____

3. Write the names of the dogs in order from the smallest to the largest?
   _____
   _____

4. Why was this piece written? _____
   _____

An Unusual Pet

Do you have a pet dog or cat? Maybe you have a pet bird or fish. But do you have a chameleon? Some families do!

A chameleon is a reptile. Like all reptiles, it has scaly skin. A chameleon has two interesting body parts. It has a long, sticky tongue. When the chameleon sees an insect, its tongue can fly out and back in less than a second. A chameleon can also change the color of its skin. The color of the skin helps it hide from enemies.

Chameleons usually live in the wild. But they can make great pets, too. Chameleons need special care. They should live in a cage made of screens. The cage should be filled with plants. Chameleons need a heat light. It warms their bodies so they can move around.

Chameleons eat crickets, moths, and flies. They can eat up to 20 bugs a day. Pet chameleons need moist air for their skin. They also need water to drink. Most people find ways to drip water slowly into the chameleon's cage.

Like any pet, a chameleon needs attention. Some chameleons are friendlier than others. They liked to be held and played with. The more they are held, the friendlier they are.

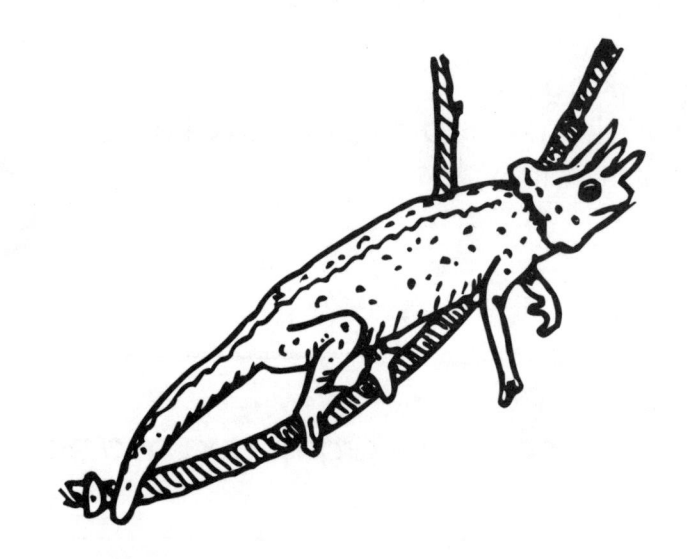

1. A chameleon is a _____ that has scaly skin.

2. Chameleons live in the wild, or they can be _____.

3. Chameleons need water to drink and water for their _____.

4. Like all pets, chameleons need _____ to be friendly.

Math   Name _____   Date _____

Pet Survey

Directions: Read the story. Then answer the questions on page 70.

Mr. Arnold turned to his class. "How many of you have pets?" he asked. Most of the students raised their hands. "Today we are going to do a survey about pets. A survey is when you ask a group of people questions. The information you get from the survey is called data. Data helps people make decisions. We will take a survey about the kinds of pets the students in this class have."

Student's Pets in Mr. Arnold's Class

Kinds of Pets	Number
Dogs	||||| ///
Cats	||||| ||||| //
Bird	////
Fish	///// /
Hamsters	//
Iguanas	X
No Pets	///

Math　　　Name _____　　　Date _____

Pet Survey (cont.)

1. How many students have fish?
   _____

2. Which pet do most students have?
   _____

3. How many more students have dogs than birds?
   _____

4. Use the information from the tally chart on page 69 to complete the bar graph below.

Student's Pets in Mr. Arnold's Class

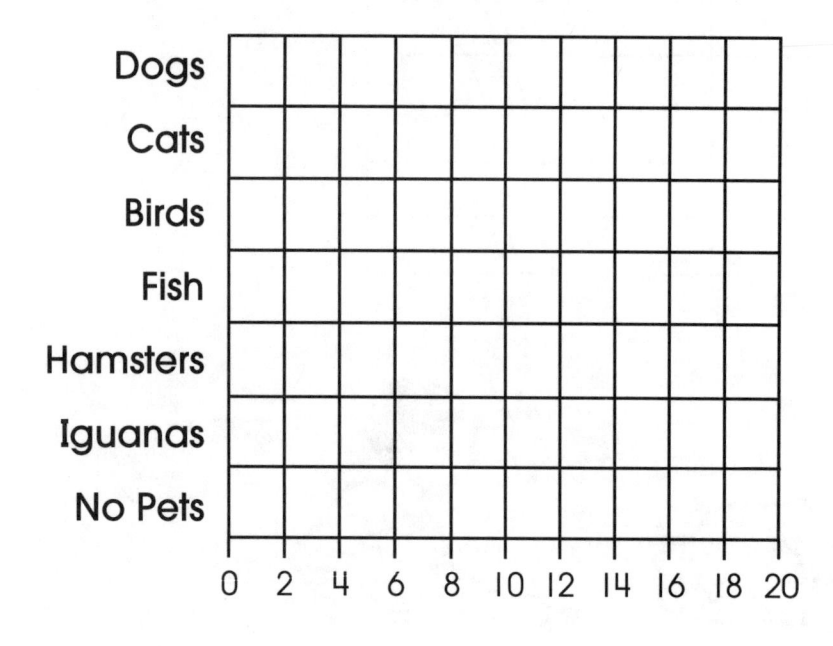

	0	2	4	6	8	10	12	14	16	18	20
Dogs											
Cats											
Birds											
Fish											
Hamsters											
Iguanas											
No Pets											

Arts

Pet Pictures

Wausau, Wisconsin

The local museum is pleased to announce a new art show. It will show the photographs of William Wegman. Wegman is best known for his humorous pictures of Weimaraners. Weimaraners, large, gray dogs, were once used for hunting animals such as deer and bears.

Wegman's photographs are one of a kind. His subjects are dressed in costumes, clothes, and masks.

One photo shows a dog dressed as Cinderella. This work and others are featured in a Cinderella storybook. Wegman's work is fresh and original.

Now you can see for yourself the creativity of Wegman's photographs. Many new works will be featured.

1. What is a Weimaraner?
   a. a dog
   b. another name for Cinderella
   c. a photograph
   d. a museum

2. In the article, what kind of art does William Wegman do?
   a. writes stories
   b. carves wood
   c. paints pictures
   d. takes photographs

3. What does Wegman do with the Weimaraners?
   a. He reads them stories
   b. He dresses them in costumes.
   c. He takes them to museums.
   d. He hunts with them.

4. Which of these sentences is an opinion?
   a. This work and others are featured in a Cinderella storybook.
   b. Wegman's work is fresh and original.
   c. Many new works will be featured.
   d. Weimaraners, large, gray dogs, were once used for hunting animals such as deer and bears.

Science   Name _____   Date_____

The Speech

Julio was feeling very nervous. He was about to give a speech to the students in his school. He wanted their help on a project. Julio took a big breath and stood up. He walked to the microphone and began his speech.

"Hi. I'm Julio Martinez. Some of you might know me. Now I'm asking for your help on a project I want to start. I saw a television show about a group of macaws that live in Brazil. Macaws are blue, red, green, and yellow birds that have beautiful long tails. Some people in Brazil capture macaws and sell them as pets. So many macaws have been caught and taken out of Brazil that these birds are close to being extinct. Extinct means they are in danger of dying out. I would like to raise money to send to a wildlife park there. We can make posters to hang in the community to tell everyone what is happening in Brazil. I'm sure there are other things we can do. All of us together can make a difference.

If you want to join me, please let me know. Thank you!"

1. What was Julio doing that made him a good citizen?

   _____

   _____

2. Why are the macaws becoming extinct?

   _____

3. Why did Julio write the speech?

   _____

   _____

4. Why do you think Julio was nervous about giving the speech? How do you think he felt after he was done?

   _____

Math   Name _____   Date _____

Three-Dimensional Buildings

Directions: Read the story. Then answer the questions on page 74.

"Today we are going to talk about buildings," announced Mrs. Baxter.

"What do buildings have to do with math?" asked Terry.

"That's a good question," answered Mrs. Baxter. "Buildings are made with many kinds of figures, both flat and three-dimensional. We are going to look at the three-dimensional figures in buildings. What building shapes do you know about already?"

"My apartment building looks like a cube," said Justin.

"My house is made using two figures," added Marta. "It has a rectangular prism base and a pyramid roof."

"My grandparents went to Egypt last year," said Lara. "They sent me a postcard that showed pictures of the pyramids."

"You have named most of the three-dimensional shapes," said Mrs. Baxter. "Two are still missing."

"Some Native Americans lived in tepees," said Carl. "They were shaped like cones."

"That's right, Carl!" said Mrs. Baxter. "But there is still one more shape."

"Well, we haven't named a sphere," said Penny. "But how can you make a round building?"

"That's the last one!" smiled Mrs. Baxter. "True, a building cannot be totally round. It would roll around. But architects make a building called a dome. The building is mostly a sphere, but it has a flat base."

"I would like to see one of those," said Lara. "I bet that would be cool to live in."

Math   Name _____   Date_____

Three-Dimensional Buildings (cont.)

1. What is this story mostly about?

   _____

   _____

2. What is a three-dimensional shape?

   _____

   _____

3. Name the five shapes listed in the story. _____

   _____

   _____

4. What is the difference between a cube and a rectangular prism?

   _____

   _____

5. What is a dome? _____

   _____

6. If you were in Mrs. Baxter's class, what kind of home would you build? Draw a picture.

Snow Today, Water Tomorrow!

How would you like to sleep in a room made of ice? Do you think it would be fun to sleep on a bed made of ice, too? Maybe you would like to drink from a glass made of ice? In Canada, you can try each of these things!

From the beginning of January to the end of March, the Ice Hotel is open for business. The building is made only from ice and snow. The building and the furniture are all made of ice. You will probably want to wear a coat inside. The whole building is a chilly 25°F.

People enjoy visiting this hotel. There is so much to see and do. The hotel has a place to watch movies. There are even two art galleries. Can you guess what kind of art you will see? You guessed it—ice sculptures!

When the winter season ends, the sun warms the building and it begins to melt. The solid ice turns back into liquid, and as the sun shines, the water evaporates. The Ice Hotel is gone, but only for a while. The cold winter winds will blow again. The evaporated water will collect into clouds. The clouds will get heavy with rain. And the rain will fall …. as snow and ice!

1. How long is the Ice Hotel open for business?
    a. 1 month
    b. 3 months
    c. 5 months
    d. 12 months

2. What is the best kind of clothing to wear in the Ice Hotel?
    a. a bathing suit
    b. a shirt
    c. a heavy coat
    d. a jacket

3. Ice is water that is …?
    a. hot.
    b. a liquid.
    c. a gas.
    d. a solid.

4. Why does the hotel close each year?
    a. It melts to the ground.
    b. The workers take a vacation.
    c. People won't come when it is hot.
    d. It gets too cold inside.

Arts   Name _____   Date _____

Building Artists

Dear Diary,

I made a drawing of a house in art today. The teacher said it was really good. She said I could be an architect some day. I never heard of an architect. I asked the librarian to help me look it up on the Internet. It sounds like fun.

Architects are really artists. When painters paint a picture, they think about color, shape, and style. Architects think about all of these things and more. Architects get to plan buildings. Then they draw pictures of the buildings.

Architects draw a plan by hand. The plan is an idea to see if all rooms of a building fit together. Then architects use a computer to draw the final plan. The computer shows them what the house will look like in two views. They can see the flat drawing of all of the rooms. It looks like a map of the building. The computer can also show how the building looks in three dimensions. This view shows the walls, floor, and ceiling. The computer lets you know if something in the plan is not the right size.

It sounds as though it would take lots of time to make house plans. The librarian said she would show me how to use a computer program that can draw pictures. I'm going to check it out after school tomorrow.

1. What does an architect do?

   _____

   _____

2. How is an architect like an artist? _____

   _____

3. How does a computer help an architect?

   _____

   _____

4. What will the author probably do tomorrow?

   _____

Social Studies   Name _____   Date_____

Kinds of Houses

There are many kinds of houses. Most houses that we live in are made of different kinds of materials. You will see glass, brick, rock, and wood all in one house. But what do people do if they don't have modern building materials? These people use materials they find in nature. They do not need to pay for the materials, and the houses can be built very quickly.

Some people live on land that is mostly clay. People mix clay with water to make adobe. Their houses look like smooth mud buildings.

Other people live in a forest filled with trees. They use trees to build their houses. They use whole logs or cut the logs into planks.

Some people live on plains where there is a lot of grass. They tie bundles of grass together to make the walls and the roof of a house. Sometimes they coat the house with mud to keep out the rain and heat. Other people weave the grass together to make their houses.

Where the land is covered in snow and ice, people cut ice into blocks. They stack the blocks to make igloos.

Some people move around too much to have a permanent house. They follow herds of animals. They need houses that are easy to move and very light. They use the skins of animals to make tents.

1. An adobe house is made of _____ with water.

2. People who live on the plains make houses of _____.

3. People who live in a forest make houses out of _____.

4. People who follow animals may live in a _____ made out of animal skins.

Math   Name _____   Date _____

House Patterns

Have you ever looked at the pattern in a tile floor? It is easy to see the color patterns. But take a closer look. What figures do you see?

Many tile floors use plane figures, or polygons, to form patterns. You can see floor patterns made with squares, rectangles, and diamonds. These figures are used the most. But you can also see patterns made with triangles, hexagons, and octagons. Sometimes you can see two or more figures in the same floor pattern. The shapes fit together without leaving any space. They do not overlap either. This kind of pattern is called a tessellation.

You can find tessellations all over your house. Take a walk around.

Look inside and outside. How many patterns can you find? What plane figures are in the pattern? But look carefully—a tessellation may be right in front of you!

1. A tessellation is made when plane figures ...

    a. join together with no spaces or overlaps.
    b. are measured.
    c. make a figure that has volume.
    d. separate into different groups.

2. What are *plane* figures?

    _____
    _____

3. Which part of a house is probably NOT a tessellation?

    a. tile floor
    b. doorway
    c. brick wall
    d. window

4. Name 2 places you might see tesellations.

    _____
    _____

© McGraw-Hill Children's Publishing   0-7424-1923-1 Theme-Based Reading Comprehension

The Japanese House

Japan is a busy country. Many people live in big cities. The cities look like those you see in other modern countries. There are skyscrapers, apartment buildings, and offices. But parts of Japan still have traditional houses. They are like the houses people lived in long ago.

The traditional house in Japan is built one or two feet off the ground. Japan gets lots of rain. The house is built above the ground to help the inside stay warm and dry.

A Japanese house looks like one big room. There is not one area for eating, sleeping, or talking. The Japanese divide the room into different spaces with screens. The screens are like walls, but they move. They are made out of wood or paper.

There is very little furniture in a traditional Japanese house. People sit on the floor to eat and talk. They eat at a low table. The people sleep on the floor, too. Special mats cover the floor. These mats are called tatami. Tatami mats are made by weaving grasses together. Tatami mats must last a long time. If you visit a traditional house in Japan, remember to take off your shoes. It shows good manners!

1. In this article, what does *traditional* mean?

_____

_____

2. What might happen if the Japanese built their houses on the ground?

_____

_____

3. Why do visitors take their shoes off in a Japanese house?

_____

_____

4. Would you like to live in a Japanese house? Why or why not?

_____

_____

That's Electricity

The milk is cold. The television is on. The lights are bright. All of these comforts in a house are possible because of electricity.

Electricity is a kind of energy. It is made from burning goal or gas. It is also made from wind and water power. This energy is stored in large machines. These machines are called generators. Generators push the energy through wires to our houses.

To get the electricity to work in a house, the energy needs a circuit. A circuit is a path the energy moves along. It moves from the wires to the wall sockets. From the sockets, the energy moves to the appliances. The switches and the buttons on appliances open and close the circuits. When a switch is open, electricity moves in a circle through the wire. The appliance will work. When the switch is closed, the electricity stops. The appliance will not work.

The next time you flip a switch to turn on a light, you will have opened a circuit. That's electricity!

1. Electricity is a kind of ...
    a. gas.
    b. energy.
    c. machine.
    d. switch.

2. What does electricity need to work?
    a. a circuit
    b. a light
    c. a store
    d. a house

3. When the light is on ...
    a. the circuit is wet.
    b. the circuit is hot.
    c. the circuit is closed.
    d. the circuit is open.

4. What happens when you push the *On* button of the stove?
    a. The heat goes off.
    b. The food gets cold.
    c. The food heats.
    d. The timer starts.

Math   Name _____   Date _____

Julie's Budget

Julie had a birthday, and her grandparents sent her a $15 check.

"What are you going to do with it?" asked her father.

"I'm not sure," answered Julie.

"Your mother and I make a family budget each month," said Mr. Garcia. "A budget is a plan that shows how we want to spend our money."

"That sounds like a good idea," said Julie. "I'll make a budget, too."

Julie made this budget.

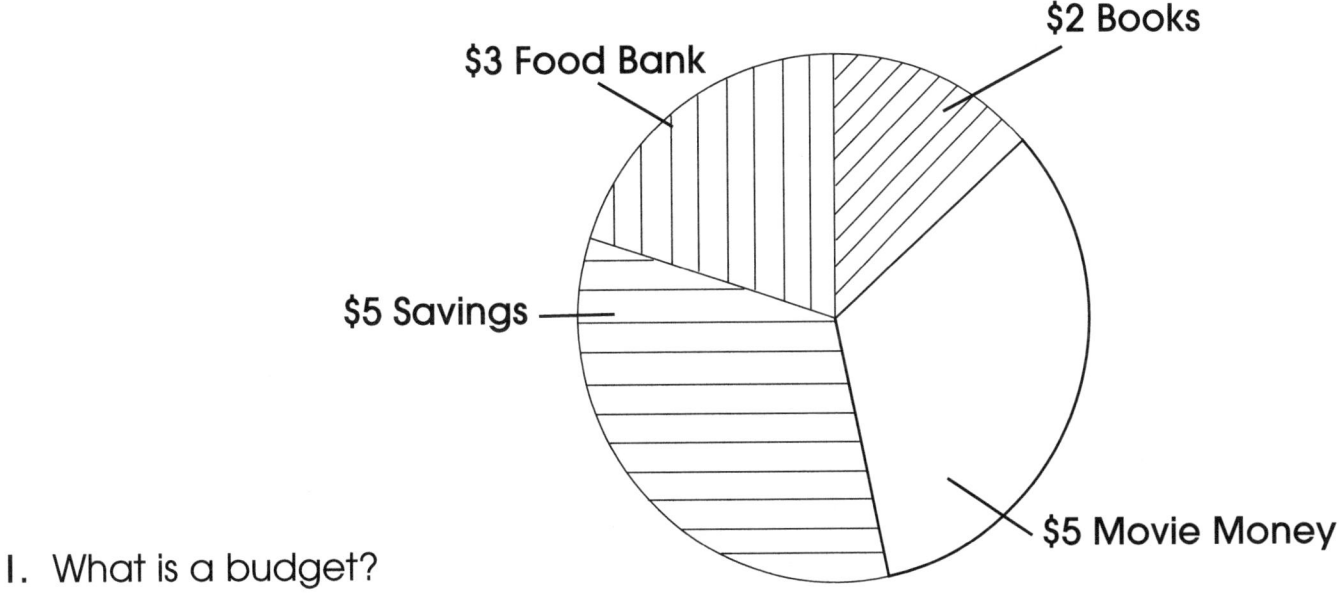

$2 Books
$3 Food Bank
$5 Savings
$5 Movie Money

1. What is a budget?

   _____

   _____

2. How much did Julie plan to save?

   _____

3. How much more money did Julie plan to spend on movies than on books?

   _____

4. If you had $15, what would your budget look like? Draw a pie chart.

Social Studies   Name _____   Date _____

Time to Vote

Gino stood in line with his mother. He watched people stand in front of tall desks. His mother called them booths. People did not talk. Everyone was very serious. They looked as though they were writing.

"Why doesn't anyone talk?" asked Gino.

"They're voting," answered his mother. "Voting is an important responsibility. We are choosing a person who will make good decisions. The people we choose need to lead our country."

"Do I get to vote today?" Gino asked.

"You must be an adult to vote," said his mother. "Voting is something a good citizen does."

"We've talked about being good citizens at school," said Gino. "I try to be a good citizen by helping my classmates."

"You do a great job helping Mr. West with his lawn, too," smiled his mother. "I'm sure when you are an adult, you'll be a good citizen by voting."

"I will!" said Gino. "I can't wait!"

1. Voting is an important _____.

2. Why should we choose a person who makes good decisions?
   _____
   _____

3. What are two ways Gino is a good citizen now?
   _____
   _____

4. List two ways you are a good citizen.
   _____
   _____

Social Studies   Name _____   Date _____

Growing Up

Dear Dad,

I'm having a great time with Grandma. We have gone biking and swimming every day. Grandma showed me photos of you growing up.

Grandma showed me what you looked like when you were a baby. She said it was the only time in your life when you held still. Then I saw photos of you as a toddler. I laughed when I saw a picture of you trying to walk. Your face was covered with cookie crumbs.

There was a picture of you, riding a bike when you were four. Grandma said you were the only kid your age who could ride a two-wheeler.

But I really liked the pictures that showed you playing baseball when you were a teenager. I didn't know you were a good pitcher. From now on, there will be no more excuses about not pitching balls to me so I can practice batting.

I think I'll start taking pictures of the whole family. I can send some to Grandma so she can see how much we all have grown.

I'll be home soon!

Love,

Dinah

1. Why did the author write this letter? _____

2. What stages of life did the author write about? _____

3. Who are the main characters in this story? _____

4. Do you think Dinah and her dad will practice batting when she gets home? Why or why not? _____

The Family Portrait

Carla wiggled in her chair. Her feet hurt from the shiny shoes. Her head hurt because her ponytail was too tight. And Carla didn't like wearing dresses. She wanted to be back in her jeans and tennis shoes.

"How much longer?" Carla asked.

"We must wait our turn before we go into the studio," said Mrs. Edwards. "The photographer should be out any minute. Then we can go into the room where all the cameras are. We'll have our portrait taken in there."

"We do a family portrait every year," said Carla. "Can't we skip this year?"

Mrs. Edwards looked at her daughter and shook her head. "You children change so quickly. I want to make sure I get a picture of our family every year," she said. "It only takes a few minutes. If you lived long ago, you would have had your portrait painted. It could have taken months. You would have had to stand still for several hours at a time. And don't forget, back then girls wore dresses all the time."

"I guess I can wait a little longer," sighed Carla. She gave her head a little scratch. Another couple of minutes wouldn't hurt.

1. Where was Carla? _____

2. What is a portrait? _____
_____

3. How are portraits today different from portraits made long ago?
_____
_____

4. Why did Carla decide that having a family portrait taken was not so bad after all? _____
_____

Social Studies   Name _____   Date _____

Happy Kwanzaa!

"Nikki, it's time to set the table," called Mother.

Nikki raced into the room. It was the first time she was old enough to celebrate Kwanzaa. It was a time to think about her family and their African traditions. They told stories about Africa. They talked about ways they could help the community. On the last night, the whole family got together. Grandpa and Grandma would come, too. They would have a big feast. There would be singing and dancing.

"I'll get the straw mat and the kinara," said Mother. "Would you please get the corn and fruit? These things help us remember that Kwanzaa is a harvest celebration in Africa."

"How many ears of corn should I get?" asked Nikki.

"Two," replied Mother. "We need an ear of corn for each child in the family."

Nikki watched as Mother placed the candles in the kinara.

"What do the candles stand for?" asked Nikki.

"We will light one candle each night," answered Mother. "The three red candles stand for the blood of the African people. The one black candle stands for the face of our people. And the three green candles stand for hope in the future."

"The table is almost done," said Nikki. "I can't wait until December 26. It's not much longer."

Kwanzaa

1. What is this story mostly about? _____

2. What do people think about during Kwanzaa? _____

3. How would the items set on the table remind people of a harvest celebration? _____

4. How many candles are in a kinara? _____

Math   Name _____   Date _____

David Goes to Work

David had only $8.27. It just wasn't enough money to buy his mother a birthday present. He needed at least $15. David wanted to buy a necklace he knew she wanted.

David walked outside and sat on the step. He watched his dad rake leaves.

"You look sad," his dad said.

"I saw something special I wanted to buy Mom for her birthday," David said. "But I don't have enough money."

"You could help with yard work," his dad suggested. "I'll pay you $2.00 to move the leaves to the compost pile. Then I'll pay you $0.50 to turn the compost pile over."

David's face brightened. "That would be great!"

David set to work. He got the wheelbarrow and another rake. He quickly loaded the leaves and wheeled them to the compost pile. David wondered whether his father might have another job for him to do. David saw his neighbor, Mrs. Stilham, and waved.

"You look as though you're doing a good job," called Mrs. Stilham. "How would you like to come help me rake leaves tomorrow? I'll pay you $4.00."

"I'll come over right after school."

1. Why did David need money?

_____

2. At the beginning of the story, how much more money did David need to buy his mother the necklace? Show your work.

_____

3. After working for his dad and Mrs. Stilham, will David have enough money to buy his mother's present? Show your work.

_____

_____

Arts

The Totem Pole

Come visit British Columbia, Canada. You will see some very interesting places. You might like to see the world's largest totem pole. It is over 80 feet (24 m) tall. A totem pole is a tree that is carved from top to bottom with animal faces. The animal faces are called totems. The animal faces are symbols of a Native-American clan. Each clan has its own symbol. Some clans have names like the bear clan or the eagle clan.

A long time ago only the most important clans made totem poles. Skilled workers carved a tree with the clan's symbol. When the totem pole was done, the clan had a potlatch. A potlatch was big party. It lasted several days. The people ate, sang, and danced. The people who gave the party passed out gifts to show their wealth. Planting the totem pole was part of the celebration.

1. Why did the author write this article?

   _____

   _____

2. What do you think a clan is? _____

   _____

3. How did you find your answer for #2?

   _____

   _____

4. What did people do to show their wealth?

   _____

   _____

Social Studies   Name _____   Date _____

A Family

A family is a group of people. These people are related. This means families are joined together. Many families are made when children are born. Other families are made when children are adopted. Still other families are made when two people get married.

At one time, most families were made of a mother, a father, and children. Today a family can be any group that is related. Some families are made of one grandparent and a child. Some families have just one parent and children. Still, some families have both parents and children. In a family, the adults give food and clothes. They also give love.

1. What is a family?
    a. people who are related
    b. people who care
    c. people who work
    d. people who talk

2. Which of the following is NOT a family?
    a. a mother and a son
    b. a mother and a friend
    c. an aunt and an uncle
    d. a grandmother and a granddaughter

3. What does the adult in a family give?
    a. clothes and songs
    b. food, clothes, and love
    c. food and friends
    d. love and songs

4. Why did the author write this article?
    a. to make sure all people belong to a family
    b. to get people to join a family
    c. to make people in families laugh
    d. to give information about a family

Language Arts   Name _____   Date _____

Mr. Nobody
by Anonymous

I know a funny little man,
As quiet as a mouse,
Who does the mischief that is done
In everybody's house!

No one ever sees his face,
And yet we all agree
That every plate was cracked
By Mr. Nobody.

'Tis he who always tears our books,
Who leaves the door ajar.
He pulls the buttons from our shirts
And scatters pins afar.
The noisy door will always squeak
For, prithee, don't you see,
We leave the oiling to be done
By Mr. Nobody.

The marks upon the door
By none of us are made;
We never leave the blinds unclosed
To let the curtains fade;
And finally, the boots
That lying 'round you see
Are not our boots;
They all belong to Mr. Nobody!

1. Who is Mr. Nobody?
   _____
   _____

2. When does Mr. Nobody show up in the house? _____
   _____

3. Why might someone say, "Mr. Nobody did it"?
   _____

4. Does Mr. Nobody live at your house? Explain.
   _____
   _____

Social Studies   Name _____   Date _____

Many Kinds of Communities

If you look up community in the dictionary, you'll find three meanings. The first meaning tells about the kind of community you find in a town or city. In this community, people live and work together. The community has everything people need to live. There are stores to buy goods and food. There are places to play and have fun. There are places to work. Some people have special jobs to make the community a safe place.

People can be part of another kind of community. In this community, people join a group. The group may share a similar interest or work at the same kind of job. In this kind of community, people do not live close together. People who paint may join with other painters to make a group. They make an art community. They take painting classes together or visit art museums.

In the world of nature, there is another kind of community. This community is made up of plants and animals that live in one area. They need each other to live. A pond is an example of a nature community. The pond animals cannot live anywhere else. They need the water and plants in the pond. Animals need very special communities.

1. How is a community that people live in like a community that animals live in? _____

_____

_____

2. What kind of people would be part of a music community? What might they do together? _____ _____

3. What kind of community would a fish belong to?

_____

_____

4. Why did the author write this article? _____

_____

_____

© McGraw-Hill Children's Publishing   0-7424-1923-1 *Theme-Based Reading Comprehension*

An Ant Community

Wes and Eric were walking through the park. An anthill was in Wes's path. He kicked it with his toe as he walked by.

"Hey, don't do that!" exclaimed Eric. "You're hurting the ants."

"Who cares about ants?" said Wes. "They'll just build it again."

"True, but how would you like it if somebody stepped on your house?" argued Eric. "Hundreds of ants have worked to dig out tunnels and rooms. Besides, it is not very kind to hurt anything in nature."

"They have rooms in there?" asked Wes.

"The queen has her own room. It is the largest one in the ant nest," Eric answered. "There are rooms for babies when they hatch from eggs. The workers have rooms where they can rest. An anthill even has a separate room for storing food."

"Wow! I didn't know an ant nest was that big," said Wes.

"It gets bigger all the time" continued Eric. "Workers are always digging new rooms and tunnels. An ant community is always growing."

"Thanks for telling me about ants," said Eric. "I'll be more careful."

1. This story is mainly about ...
   a. friends walking in the park.
   b. parts of an anthill.
   c. how to kick anthills.
   d. what worker ants do.

2. Which of the following is NOT a room in an anthill?
   a. a king's room
   b. a room for babies
   c. a food store
   d. a resting room

3. Why do workers build new rooms?
   a. The old rooms fill up with dirt.
   b. Children always kick them over.
   c. The babies need a place to play.
   d. The ant community keeps growing.

4. The next time Wes sees an anthill he will ...
   a. leave it alone.
   b. kick it.
   c. dig it up.
   d. show it to Eric.

Social Studies   Name _____   Date _____

It's the Law

A community has many laws. A law is like a rule. Laws help keep everyone safe. There are laws for driving cars and riding bikes. There are laws for ways to act in buildings and parks. There are even laws for making laws.

Many towns have a mayor, who helps make laws. A mayor has an important job. The mayor is in charge of the town. This person makes sure the town is a safe and fair place to live. The mayor usually has a group of people who help him or her make the laws. These people make up the mayor's council. The people in the community can also help shape the laws. Before the mayor makes a law, the town calls a meeting. People in the community tell what they think about the new law. After people talk, the mayor and council vote. The law becomes another rule when most of the council and the mayor vote for it.

1. A _____
   is a rule that keeps everyone safe.

2. A _____
   is in charge of a town.

3. A _____
   is a group of people who helps the mayor make laws.

4. At a meeting, people in the _____
   tell what they think about a new law.

A Chain of Life

Directions: Read the article. Then answer the questions on page 94.

There are many kinds of communities in nature. Forests, deserts, and oceans are examples of special nature communities. In a nature community, animals and plants live together. They need each other to live.

A food chain shows how the plants and animals need each other. Let's take a look at a forest food chain. Most food chains begin with plants. The forest food chain is no different. There are lots of leaves and grasses in the forest. Animals that eat plants are the next link in the chain. Mice, squirrels, and rabbits eat plants. Next, the animals that eat meat are the third link in the chain. An owl and a skunk prey on smaller animals. Finally, bigger animals hunt the owl and skunk. A fox is another link in the food chain.

Food chains can be broken. Suppose all of the mice get sick. If there are not any mice, what does an owl eat? The owl would go hungry. Or what might happen to an owl that eats a sick mouse? The owl might get sick, too. Most animals eat several kinds of foods. So if one part of the chain breaks, The animals can eat other animals. But some animals eat only one kind of food. For example, a panda eats only a special kind of bamboo. If the bamboo dies, the panda dies, too.

It's very important to keep each part of the food chain healthy. A break in the chain can break a community.

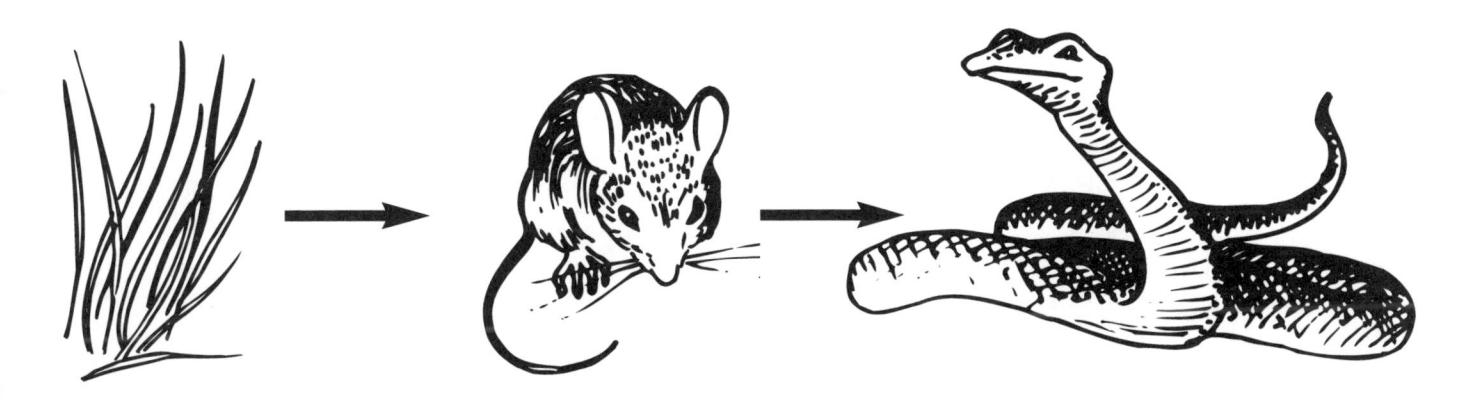

A Chain of Life (cont.)

1. Which of the following is NOT a nature community?

    a. pond
    b. desert
    c. tree
    d. forest

2. A food chain shows ...

    a. what plants an animal eats.
    b. where animals live.
    c. how animals eat.
    d. how plants and animals live together.

3. What do most food chains begin with?

    a. food
    b. plants
    c. fish
    d. animals

4. In a forest food chain, which animal comes after the grass?

    a. owl
    b. fox
    c. skunk
    d. rabbit

5. What animals might be the next link after the rabbit in a forest food chain?

    a. a rabbit
    b. a human
    c. a fish
    d. a tree

6. How can a food chain be broken? _____

    _____

    _____

Community Fun

Lena was standing on an outdoor stage. She looked out from behind the curtain. She saw lots of people who lived in her town. They were sitting on blankets in the park. They were waiting for the play to begin.

Lena was excited. This was her very first time to act in the community theater. She was playing the part of person riding a bus. She had only one line to say, but it was an important one.

Lena turned and watched the other actors getting ready. The lead actor was her neighbor, Mrs. Thomas. Her teacher, Mr. Todd, was a bus rider, too. Being part of the community theater was great fun. The community theater was a group of people who lived in the town and put on shows. Only the director, who told everyone what to do, got paid. Everyone else did the show because it was fun.

"Get in your places," the director called. Lena rushed to her seat on the bus. She hoped she would remember her line.

1. Where was the stage in the story?
   a. in an auditorium
   b. in a park
   c. in a store
   d. in a bus

2. What did Lena do after looking at the people waiting for the show to begin?
   a. She talked to the director.
   b. She talked to her teacher.
   c. She sat on the bus.
   d. She watched the other actors get ready.

3. A community theater is ...
   a. a group of people in the community who like to watch plays.
   b. a group of people in the community who like to act in plays.
   c. a place in the community that talks about plays.
   d. a place in the community where people watch plays.

4. What do you think will happen next in the story?
   a. Lena will go to school.
   b. The bus will leave.
   c. The actors will leave.
   d. The play will begin.

Math   Name _____   Date _____

Vacation Weather

City	January Temp (°F)	April Temp (°F)	July Temp (°F)	October Temp (°F)	Rain (in.)	Snowfall (in.)
Anchorage, Alaska	13.0	13.0	58.1	34.6	15.20	69.2
Reno, Nevada	32.2	46.4	69.5	50.3	7.49	25.3
Tampa, Florida	59.8	71.5	82.1	74.4	46.73	0.0

1. Do you think it would be a good idea to go to Alaska in April? Why or why not? _____

2. Do you think you could ski in Nevada in April? Why or why not? _____

3. Would you like to visit friends in Florida in April? Why or why not? _____

4. Where would you like to go on vacation and why? _____

The Mural Contest

Enter the Mural Contest!

The mayor is asking for your help. She wants to make the town of Westville a beautiful place to live. Mayor Grant wants a mural to be painted on the side of the post office. This large picture will show why Westville is special. Mayor Grant wants people to make pictures of their ideas. Store owners will choose the best picture. All members of the community are asked to join the fun. They can draw a mural idea or help paint the building.

1. What is a mural? _____

2. Why would a mural make a community look better? _____

3. What are two ways members of the community can help with the mural? _____

4. Suppose your community made a mural. What pictures would you want on it that showed how your town was special? _____

Social Studies   Name _____   Date _____

Communities Here and There

Look at the drawing. Then answer the questions about this community.

1. Is this community probably in the country or the city?
   _____

2. Do you think this community is near where you live? Why or why not?
   _____
   _____

3. Write three facts about what you observe in this community.
   _____
   _____
   _____

4. Compare this community to yours. Write in the Venn diagram.

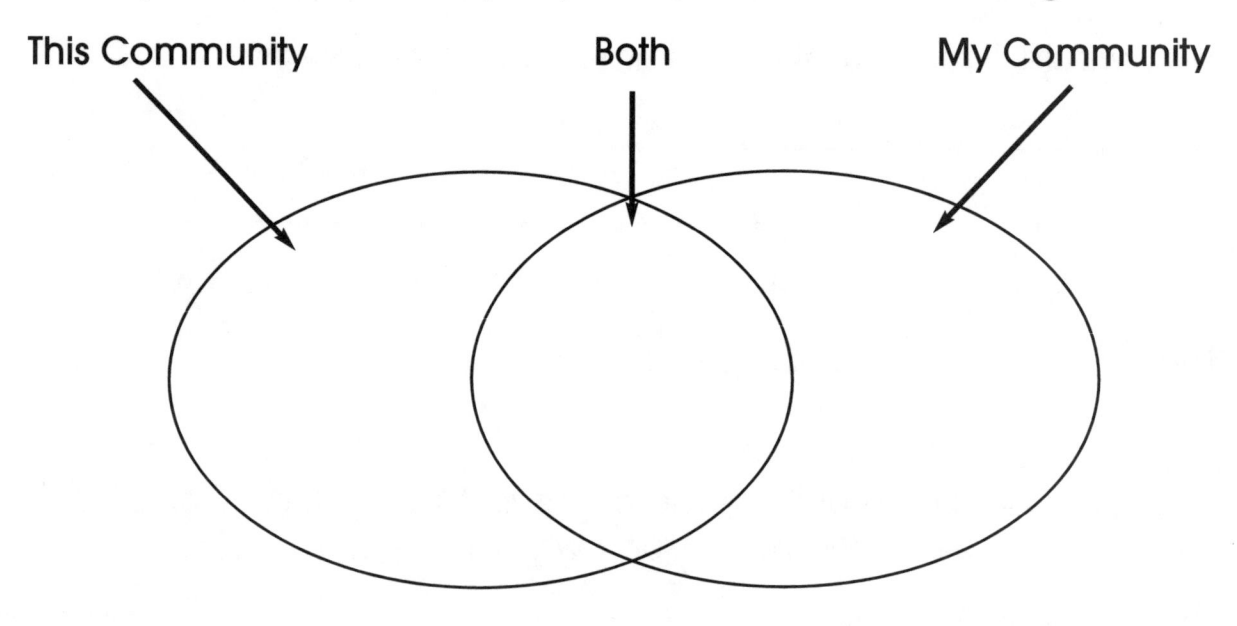

This Community   Both   My Community

Language Arts/Social Studies Name_____ Date_____

Why Bears Hibernate in Winter: A Native-American Folktale

Directions: Read the story. Then answer the questions on page 100.

Bear stood at the top of a hill and shouted, "I'm the biggest, strongest animal in the woods!" Then he raced down the hill. Bear stopped by the lake at the bottom of the hill. "I'm the fastest animal, too" he boasted.

Turtle looked up at him through a hole in the ice. "You may be the biggest animal in the forest, but I'm the fastest," Turtle said.

Bear laughed, "Everybody knows you're the slowest animal, Turtle."

"Well, let's have a race," answered Turtle. "You can run around the lake, and I'll swim around it."

Bear scratched his head. "There's so much ice covering the lake, how will I know if you're swimming the whole distance?" he asked.

Turtle thought for a minute. "We'll ask Elk to punch holes in the lake with his hoof. When I get to a hole, I'll poke my head up so you can see where I am."

Bear agreed to the plan. The race was set for the next day.

Elk punched holes through the ice. Then he yelled for the race to begin.

Turtle ducked under the ice, and Bear began running around the lake. Bear waved and greeted the animals he saw. Soon Turtle popped up through the ice. He was ahead of Bear!

"I'm ahead of you," Turtle called. Bear was amazed and began to run faster.

In a few more minutes, Turtle looked up through the next hole. "I'm winning!" he called. Bear began to run with all his might.

Each time Turtle poked his head through the ice, he was farther ahead of Bear. Bear was panting heavily. He quickly fell behind. There was no way Bear could catch Turtle, so he stopped running. Bear turned away from the lake and stomped back to his cave. He was so embarrassed that he slept the rest of the winter.

After all of the forest animals left, Turtle tapped on the ice. A turtle head popped up through each hole.

"Dear brothers and sisters, I thank you for your help," said Turtle. "We may not be fast, but we're very smart!"

To this day, bears hibernate during the winter so they don't have to remember the day they lost the race.

Language Arts/Social Studies Name _____ Date_____

Why Bears Hibernate in Winter: A Native-American Folktale (cont.)

1. What did Bear boast about? _____
   _____

2. Why did the animals of the forest want Turtle to win the race?
   _____
   _____

3. What happened after Elk punched holes in the ice?
   _____
   _____

4. Why did Bear leave the race before it was over?
   _____
   _____

5. How did Turtle win the race?
   _____
   _____

6. Do you think Turtle won the race fairly? Why or why not?
   _____
   _____

7. Do you think Bear will boast anymore? Why or why not?
   _____
   _____

Language Arts   Name _____   Date _____

The March Wind
by Anonymous

I come to work as well as play;
I'll tell you what I do.
I whistle all the live-long day,
"Woo-oo-oo-oo! Woo-oo!"

I toss the branches up and down
And shake them to and fro;
I whirl the leaves in flocks of brown
And send them high and low.

I strew the twigs upon the ground,
The frozen earth I sweep;
I blow the children round and round
And wake the flowers from sleep.

1. Why is this poem called "The March Wind"?

   _____

   _____

2. How does the wind "play"?

   _____

   _____

3. What does the phrase "The frozen earth I sweep" mean?

   _____

   _____

4. How can you tell that spring is on its way?

   _____

   _____

Math/Science   Name _____   Date_____

How Far Away?

Mia and Ben sat on the porch in the late spring. Dark clouds were building up in the west. A flash of lightning streaked in the sky.

Ben started counting slowly, "1, 2, 3, 4 …"

"Why are you counting?" asked Mia.

"I want to see how far away the storm is," Ben answered.

"How does counting help?" Mia asked.

"A flash of lightning and the sound of thunder happen at the same time," said Ben. "You can't always hear the thunder, though. If the lightning is more then 10 miles away, you won't hear the thunder. As the storm gets closer, you can begin to hear the thunder. At first, it makes a low rumble. As the storm moves closer, the thunder gets louder and becomes a short, loud clap. To find out the storm distance, slowly count until you hear thunder. Then multiply by 1,200 to find out how far away it is. Sound travels at close to 1,200 feet (36 m) per second in warmer temperatures."

"There's a flash of light," exclaimed Mia. "1, 2, 3, 4. The storm is about 4 seconds away. I don't think I need to multiply to know that the storm is really close. We'd better go inside."

1. What happens at the same time lightning strikes?

   _____

2. Why can't you always hear thunder?

   _____

3. How far away was the thunderstorm when Mia counted? Show your work. _____

   _____

4. There are 5,280 feet in a mile. Was the thunderstorm more than a mile away or less than a mile away? Show your work.

   _____

Science   Name _____   Date _____

Make a Tornado

A tornado is the most dangerous storm on earth. The winds of a tornado can reach speeds of 300 miles per hour. You can make a model of a tornado to see how it works.

You will need:

glass jar with a lid
food coloring
dish soap
water
teaspoon

1. Fill the glass jar $\frac{3}{4}$ full of water.
2. Add several drops of food coloring.
3. Add one teaspoon of dish soap.
4. Put the lid on the jar.
5. Shake the jar for about 30 seconds.
6. Set the jar on the table with your hand on the top of the jar.
7. Quickly twist the jar.

1. What is the most dangerous storm on earth?
   a. a blizzard
   b. a hurricane
   c. a thunderstorm
   d. a tornado

2. A tornado is ...
   a. a thunderstorm.
   b. a sandstorm.
   c. a windstorm.
   d. a rainstorm.

3. What do you do after putting the lid on the jar?
   a. Shake the jar.
   b. Add dish soap.
   c. Look at the jar.
   d. Twist the jar.

4. How is this experiment a model?
   a. It is a copy of something larger that is real.
   b. It is a recipe.
   c. It tells how to do something.
   d. It is a kind of art.

Social Studies   Name _____   Date_____

Ellie's Favorite Season

Ellie came running into the park. She raced up to her friends and skidded to a halt. "Guess what season starts today," she panted.

Rodney looked at her strangely. "It's spring," he answered. "And the season started last month in March."

"No, silly," answered Ellie. "It's baseball season! It's time for the major league teams to begin practicing. I can't wait!"

Rodney and Beth laughed. "Only you would know that," said Beth.

"You bet I do," smiled Ellie. "I follow all of the teams. There are 30 baseball teams in all. There are 162 games this year, and I want to watch them all."

"That's a lot of games," said Beth. "I'm glad we play only 30 games during our baseball season."

"Some teams play more games," said Ellie. "The baseball season may end, but the best teams get to go to the playoffs. I hope the Yankees win the pennant in October. They are my favorite team."

1. When does the baseball season begin?
   _____

2. When does the baseball season end? How do you know?
   _____

3. Do you think Beth plays baseball? Why or why not?
   _____.

4. Why did the author write this story?
   _____
   _____

5. Name two other sports seasons. _____
   _____

Science   Name _____   Date _____

Animals Adapt

Africa has two main seasons—a wet season and a dry season. During the dry season, it is very hot. The waters of lakes and ponds dry up. Some of the animals that live in the water have interesting ways to adapt to this season. They slow their breathing and their heartbeat. The other parts of their bodies slow down, too.

The lungfish is one animal that is able to live through the dry season. The lungfish looks like an eel. While it is a fish that lives in water, it needs air to breathe. When the water of the pond dries up, the lungfish digs deep into the mud. All parts of its body slow down. The lungfish stays buried until the pond fills with water.

1. What do you think the wet season of Africa might be like?

   _____

   _____

2. How do some water animals adapt to dry ponds and lakes?

   _____

   _____

3. How is a lungfish different from other fish?

   _____

   _____

4. How does slowing down their body parts help animals stay alive?

   _____

   _____

Science   Name _____   Date_____

Monsoon Winds

Monsoons are strong winds that blow near the Indian Ocean and Asia. These winds happen two times a year. They cause two very different monsoon seasons for the people of the area.

One monsoon seasons happens in summer. The winds blow in from the ocean across the land. The ocean air is moist. Clouds form over the land in the summer heat nearly every day. The area gets large amounts of rain. Some places get so much rain that the crops are ruined. There are times when rivers rise above the banks and flood towns.

The second monsoon season begins in the winter. The wind moves in the opposite direction from the summer monsoon. The wind blows from the land to the ocean. It is a dry wind and does not affect the life of the people.

1. _____ is a strong wind that blows near the Indian Ocean.

2. The monsoon wind that blows in the _____ moves from the ocean to the land.

3. The moist ocean air causes large amounts of _____.

4. The winter monsoon is a _____ wind.

Science   Name _____   Date _____

The Climate Seasons

Spring, summer, fall, and winter are the climate seasons. Climate is the weather and temperature of a place. During the seasons, the climate changes.

Spring happens during the months of March, April, and May. The first part of the season is cool and windy. By the end of the season, the days are warmer. Many places get lots of rain. Plants begin to grow during this time. The daylight lasts longer.

Summer follows spring and lasts the months of June, July, and August. It is the hottest time of the year. Some places see temperatures over 100°F (38°C) for many days. Nights are very warm, too. Plants have finished growing and are producing food. Daylight can last almost 15 hours.

Cooler winds blow during the fall months of September, October, and November. The days are cool and pleasant, but the nights can be cold. Fall is the time to harvest crops, and many trees lose their leaves. The hours of daylight are the same as the spring.

The last climate season is winter. It lasts during the months of December, January, and February. Cold winds blow, so temperatures are colder in most places. Snow can fall and may stay on the ground when the temperatures stay below 32°F. Plants do not grow during this time. The sun rises later and sets earlier, so the hours of daylight are very short.

1. This article is mostly about ...
    a. the changes in the seasons.
    b. the months of the seasons.
    c. plant growth.
    d. heat and rain.

2. Climate is ...
    a. the hours the light shines.
    b. the amount of rain a place gets.
    c. the months in a year.
    d. the weather and temperature.

3. Which season has hot, dry weather?
    a. spring
    b. summer
    c. fall
    d. winter

4. Which season does the picture above show?
    a. spring
    b. summer
    c. fall
    d. winter

Social Studies   Name _____   Date _____

Gung Hay Fat Choy!

Gung Hay Fat Choy! This is the greeting that people in China call to each other during the Chinese New Year. It is a wish for a happy and wealthy year. The Chinese New Year is a huge holiday. It lasts three days. However, there is a lot to do to get ready for this important holiday.

The preparation begins about two weeks before the Chinese New Year. People buy presents. They paint their windows and doors red. They clean their houses from top to bottom to sweep away bad feelings. They also make special food and buy new clothes.

Then, on the night of the New Year, friends and family gather for a huge feast. Fireworks light up the sky at midnight. Everyone is joyful.

1. What do people wish for others at the new year?
   _____

2. Name three things people do to get ready for the new year.
   _____
   _____

3. What happens on New Year's night?
   _____
   _____

4. What do you think is the best part of the Chinese New Year?
   _____

Science   Name _____   Date_____

Insects—One Big Happy Group

Insects are fun to watch. Most times of the year you can see them racing from one place to another. They all look different though. Do you know what special parts these animals have that make them one big group? Let's find out!

First, all insects have a hard outside shell. They do not have bones to give them shape. It is the exoskeleton that keeps their inside parts safe.

Next, insects have three main body sections. The head is the first section. The head has the eyes and mouth. An insect also has two antennas. Antennas are the feelers of an insect. They help the insect smell and learn about the wind conditions before they fly. The second body section is the thorax. Here you can see the body parts that help the insect move. All insects have six legs. Some insects have wings. The abdomen is the last section. It looks as though has many parts joined together. In most insects, the abdomen is the biggest part of the body.

Now you know about insects. See if you can find several different kinds. Then find all at the parts that make insects one big happy group.

1. What is an exoskeleton?
   a. a kind of insect
   b. a kind of bone
   c. something to feel with
   d. a hard outside shell

2. How many legs does an insect have?
   a. 2
   b. 4
   c. 6
   d. 8

3. What parts are on the thorax of the insect?
   a. those that help the insect eat
   b. those that help the insect sleep
   c. those that help the insect move
   d. those that help the insect see

4. Where is the antenna?
   a. on the leg
   b. on the head
   c. on the thorax
   d. on the wing

© McGraw-Hill Children's Publishing   0-7424-1923-1 *Theme-Based Reading Comprehension*

Math/Science

Insect Record Holders

My name is Zant Ant, and I live in an anthill by a running track.

My insect friends and I love the springtime because this place gets busy. You run and jump in different sports events at a track meet. We wish we could join you in these games. We would beat you in almost every track event.

For example, you think that jumping 29 feet (8 m) for a long jump is good. For humans, I'm sure it's close to a record. But you really should think about my friend Grasshopper. He can jump 30 inches (76 cm). If you think about the size of his body and how far he jumps, that is a long distance. To equal that jump, you humans would have to leap from one end of a football field to the other.

My friend Flea wants to give the high jump a try. We've seen you humans jump just over 7 feet (2 m). Flea thinks she is better. Flea can jump into the air almost 4 feet (1 m). You humans would have to jump half a mile (.8 km) to equal the same distance.

And I don't want to brag, but I'm pretty strong. I know there is a sports event where humans lift weights. It doesn't matter who holds the weight-lifting record. I know I can beat you. I can lift 50 times the weight of my body, and I do it with my mouth. Can you?

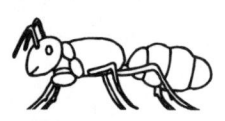

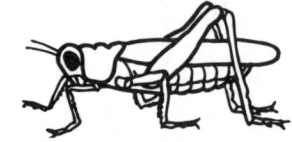

1. How is this story real? How is it make-believe?

   _____

   _____

2. A grasshopper jumps about 30 times its body length. How far could you jump if you were a grasshopper?

   _____

3. How far would a human have to jump to equal the jump of a flea?

   _____

4. How much would you have to lift to equal the weight an ant lifts?

Arts   Name   Date

Silk-Screen Prints

People have printed on paper for many thousands of years. They cut blocks of wood to press letters and pictures onto paper. This kind of art was called woodblock printing. But there was another way people made prints. It has been used for a long time, too. This method uses silk. It is a kind of art called silk-screen printing.

To make a print, a piece of silk cloth is stretched across a wooden frame. It makes a screen. Then shapes are cut out of paper. The printer uses the shapes to make a design. The shapes are placed on the paper that is to be printed. Next, the printer puts ink on the silk screen.

A flat rubber blade is pulled across the silk screen. The blade squeezes the ink through the silk and onto the paper. The shapes on the paper block the ink. When the shapes are removed, that part of the paper is free of paint. The printer then washes the silk screen. Working with the same printed paper, the printer lays different shapes on the paper and squeezes a new color through the silk screen. It takes several layers of paint and different paper designs to make a beautiful silk-screen print.

1. What are two ways to print on paper that the story mentions?

   _____

2. How is silk-screen printing different from woodblock printing?

   _____

   _____

3. What happens after the printer puts ink on the silk screen?

   _____

   _____

4. Why do you think the silk screen needs to be washed when a different color of ink is used?

   _____

   _____

Big Bugs

Insects come in all sizes. Some, like the gnat, are so small they are hard to see. Others are bigger. You may have seen a moth with wings that spread close to 6 inches (15 cm) wide. But insects that are found in the United States are actually small. If you visit countries near the equator, you will see some really big bugs.

The weather is much warmer near the equator all year long. Many rain forests are found there. This ecosystem has lots of trees and water from rain. It is an ideal place for insects to live and grow. So how big do the bugs in a rain forest grow? Some beetles grow to almost 7 inches (18 cm) long. There is one moth whose wings measure 12 inches (30 cm) wide when they are spread. One kind of walking stick is the longest insect. It grows to over 14 inches (36 cm) long. Now that's a big bug!

1. A _____ is a kind of insect that is hard to see.

2. Insects in the United States are _____.

3. The rain forest is a good home for insects because it is warm and _____.

4. The_____ is the longest bug.

Math/Science

Butterfly Lessons

Penny and Kuo sat outside at the picnic table. They were doing math homework.

"Maybe I should go back inside," Penny said. "I won't learn about symmetry out here. It's too pretty to think about boring stuff. Who cares if something looks the same on each side of a line? Why do we need to know about symmetry anyway?"

Kuo looked at her friend. "Some people need to know about symmetry to do their jobs. A person who designs buildings or clothes needs to know about symmetry."

"I'm going to do something with science," Penny said. "Science is so much more interesting."

As Penny closed her book, a beautiful orange and black butterfly landed at the end of the table.

"Hello, Monarch butterfly," Penny called. "Look how beautiful you are!"

"And look at the symmetry on that butterfly, too!" said Kuo. "When it flies off, look at the pattern on its wings. Each side has the exact same pattern."

Penny opened her math book again. "Maybe I do need math," she sighed.

1. How did Penny feel about math? Tell why you think so.

_____

_____

2. How did Penny know what kind of butterfly landed on the table?

_____

_____

3. How did the butterfly show symmetry? _____

_____

4. Do you think Penny will continue to do her math homework outside? Why or why not? _____

A New Kind of Thermometer

Have you ever heard crickets chirp at night? Sometimes there are so many crickets that it gets really noisy! Crickets make the chirping sound by rubbing their back legs together. The sound can be very loud. It can also annoy you! Sometimes the chirping seems to last all night. But the chirping can give you some very interesting information. It can tell you the temperature!

Some scientists say you can count the chirps of a cricket to find the temperature. Crickets chirp faster as the temperature goes up. Here is what you do.

1. Listen for the sound of one cricket.
2. Count the number of chirps the cricket makes in 15 seconds.
3. Add 39 to the number of chirps. The sum is the temperature in degrees Fahrenheit.

So the next time you hear a cricket, count the chirps. You can see if this new thermometer works!

1. How do crickets make the chirping noise?
   a. with their antennas
   b. with their front legs
   c. with their back legs
   d. with their mouths

2. What do crickets do as the temperature goes up?
   a. They chirp more slowly.
   b. They chirp faster.
   c. They sing louder.
   d. They sing more quietly.

3. Which number sentence could you use to find out the temperature?
   a. chirps + 39 = temperature
   b. chirps − 39 = temperature
   c. chirps x 39 = temperature
   d. chirps ÷ 39 = temperature

4. How do you think the author feels about crickets?
   a. They annoy but interest her.
   b. They amuse her.
   c. She likes their singing.
   d. She does not like them.

Science   Name _____   Date _____

A Butterfly Life Cycle

All living things grow and change. Some things change more than others. These changes form a pattern that happens over and over again. The growth pattern is called a life cycle. A butterfly is one kind of insect that grows and changes in a life cycle.

Butterflies often lay eggs on plants. When the butterfly hatches, it looks like a worm. It does not have legs or colorful wings. Most people call this insect a caterpillar. Scientists call it a larva.

In the larva stage, the butterfly eats lots of leaves. It needs the food because it grows so fast. Soon the caterpillar stops eating. Then it spins thread around its body. The thread forms a cocoon.

Inside the cocoon, the butterfly is in the pupa stage. During this stage, the butterfly changes the most. It begins to look like adult butterfly. After several weeks, the butterfly opens the cocoon. It has completed the life cycle. It is an adult now. The butterfly sits on the edge of the cocoon to dry its wings. Then it flies away.

1. What is a life cycle? _____
   _____

2. Why does a caterpillar need so much food?
   _____
   _____

3. Label the stages in the life cycle of a butterfly.

   a. _____
   b. _____
   c. _____
   d. _____

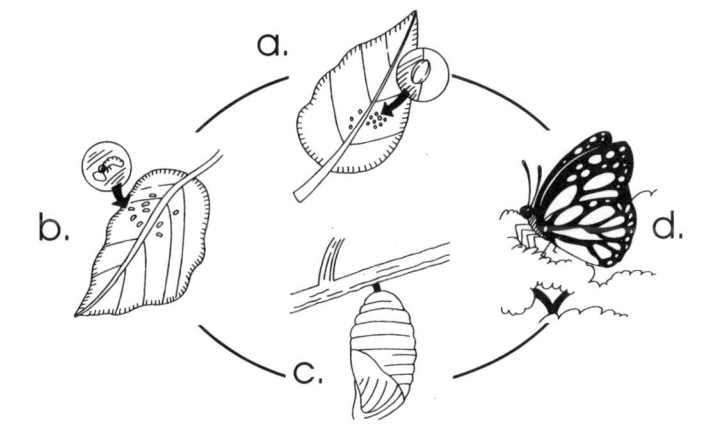

© McGraw-Hill Children's Publishing   0-7424-1923-1 Theme-Based Reading Comprehension

Language Arts/Social Studies Name _____ Date _____

The Legend of Silk

A Chinese emperor looked out into his garden. He was surprised to see a mulberry tree without leaves. The emperor called his wife and asked her to find out what had happened to the tree.

The emperor's wife walked to the garden. She found tiny white worms hungrily eating the mulberry leaves. She also saw silky white cocoons attached to some of the leaves. When the emperor's wife looked closer, she saw one of the worms spinning a white thread around its body.

The wife pulled one of the cocoons off the tree. She would take it to the emperor. He would not like these worms on his lovely tree.

On the way to see the emperor, she stopped by the kitchen. As the wife looked into a pot of boiling water, the white cocoon fell in. The cocoon spread apart.

"What a beautiful shiny thread!" the emperor's wife said.

The wife took the thread to the emperor. He agreed that it was beautiful. The wife decided to wind several of the threads together to make a stronger thread. She had an idea. What beautiful cloth this thread would make! The wife quickly ran to the emperor and asked him to plant more mulberry trees. She called the thread silk.

1. What happened after the king saw his tree without leaves?

   _____

   _____

2. What kind of tree were the worms eating?

   _____

   _____

3. What caused the cocoon to spread apart into threads?

   _____

   _____

Social Studies   Name _____   Date _____

Working to Save the Monarch Butterfly

Each year Monarch butterflies migrate south. They fly from Canada and all over the United States to go to a small town in Mexico. The butterflies return to the same town each year. They spend the winter in a forest that is warm.

The Monarch butterfly is in danger. Its forest is in trouble. A logging company has cut down many trees nearby. The butterflies face many problems without the trees. There is less food. There is not enough space for all of them to live.

Scientists have recorded the changes in Mexico. They have shown the changes to different nature groups. They have also shown the changes them to the Mexican government. The scientists are asking for help. They want to save the Monarch butterflies. The Mexican government passed several laws to protect the butterflies. They have turned more land into a park for the butterflies. They also pay people who lose their logging jobs. The nature groups are telling people about the problems the butterflies face. Together many people hope to make a difference in the life of the butterflies.

1. What does *migrate* mean?

   _____

   _____

2. Why is the forest in Mexico in danger?

   _____

   _____

3. How has the government helped the Monarch butterflies?

   _____

   _____

4. Why is it helpful to learn about the Monarch butterfly's problem?

   _____

   _____

Answer Key

Pretest .... page 8
1. The animals were arguing to see who would drink first.
2. Possible answer: He was trying to scare Lion.
3. He saw vultures flying above after he roared.
4. Possible answer: The animals would have fought, and one of the animals would probably have been hurt. The vultures would have had food.

Posttest .... page 9
1. The story is about the friendship ants and acacia trees have so they can survive in the hot, dry weather of Africa.
2. The acacia tree gives food and water to the ant as it eats the leaves.
3. The ant clears grass away from the tree that takes its water. The ant also bites animals that eat the parts of the tree.
4. Possible answer: Parts of the acacia tree would be eaten by animals, the tree might die because the nearby grass drinks the water.

Plant Cycles .... page 10
1. cycle
2. stem
3. bud
4. flower

Tree Needs .... pages 11-12
1. A plant needs sunlight, air, water, and good soil to grow.
2. Possible answer: The soil was rocky or packed down.
3. Possible answer: Plants get water when it rains and when people water them.
4. Roots take in water and air.
5. Air and water can't drain into hard soil or rocks because there are no spaces for the air and water to go.
6. Dave was saying that he needed to eat, because food has nutrients that people need to help them grow.

Memory Tree .... page 13
1. d
2. c
3. a

A "Berry" Colorful Dye .... page 14
1. After the water boils, lower the heat and simmer the mixture for 30 to 60 minutes.
2. *Strain* means to remove.
3. The amount of berries and wool are both one pound.
4. You would need 2 pounds of berries and 8 gallons of water.

The Kite-Eating Tree .... page 15
1. Possible answer: Manny's kite got caught in a tree. He and his friend Kate used proportional fractions to figure out if a ladder was tall enough to help them reach the kite.
2. Kate looked for a short tree to measure.
3. Possible answer:
   a. Find the least common multiple of both numbers:
      6: 6, 12, 18, 24, 30
      30: 30
   b. Multiple to make the fractions equivalent:
      (4 x 5)/(6 x 5) = x/30
   c. Compare the fractions:
      20/30 = x/30
4. Possible answer: They will fly the kite on the soccer field in the park.

From Forest to House .... page 16
1. Possible answer: It will need to be cut into pieces to get it down to the ground, and the wood will not be as easy to move or as valuable.
2. The log is cut into long square blocks.
3. A kiln dries out the wood.
4. The boards will twist and crack when they are nailed together.

Answer Key

Petal Patterns .... pages 17–18
1. A pattern is the repeated colors, shapes, or lines in a design.
2. Possible answer: Fibonacci was a man who found a number pattern that was repeated in plants and animals.
3. 233; 89 + 144 = 233
4. You will be amazed with this pattern in nature.
5. Possible answers: There are five leaves. Five is a number in the Fibonacci sequence. The veins in the leaves form a pattern that is parallel. Opposite leaves are attached to the stem at the same point.

A Japanese Art .... page 19
1. b
2. c
3. a
4. d

Thank You, Mr. Carver! .... page 20
1. c
2. a
3. a
4. b

Moon Festival .... page 21
1. The Moon Festival takes place on August 15.
2. China celebrates the Moon Festival.
3. They listen to poems and songs at night after the moon comes up.
4. Possible answers: Family and friends get together. It is a celebration of a good harvest. People eat lots of food.

Oh, Mister Moon .... page 22
1. It is night.
2. Possible answer: The moon is probably full because the song talks about a bright and shiny moon. The moon is bright and shiny when it is full.
3. The moon is not really hiding. It has not risen all the way in the sky.
4. The person in the song is might be going home to go to bed.

It's Just a Phase .... pages 23–24
1. a
2. d
3. c
4. b
5. c
6. a

The Science Test .... pages 25–26
1. The story is about the solar system and the order of the planets.
2. Possible answers: sun, planets, moons, stars, comets
3. Wes could not remember the names of the planets in order.
4. My very energetic mother just sent us nine pizzas.
5. a. Mercury
   b. Venus
   c. Earth
   d. Mars
   e. Jupiter
   f. Saturn
   g. Uranus
   h. Neptune
   i. Pluto

Size Counts .... page 27
1. A sphere looks like a round ball. The planets look like round balls, too.
2. (circle with horizontal line through middle)
3. Venus has about the same diameter as Earth.
4. The planet order from the smallest to the largest is Pluto, Mercury, Mars, Venus, Earth, Neptune, Uranus, Saturn, and Jupiter.

A Postcard from Rome .... page 28
1. A sculpture is a piece of stone that is carved into shapes.
2. It is in Rome, Italy.
3. Jupiter was the biggest planet, so it was named for the most important god.
4. It is a beautiful city.

Answer Key

On a Moonwalk .... page 29
1. People bounce when they walk in both places.
2. Gravity keeps things from flying into the air, and the moon doesn't have much gravity.
3. The astronauts planted an American flag.
4. Possible answer: Scientists wanted rocks and dirt so they could learn to find out more about the moon.

Going in Circles .... page 30
1. light
2. rotation
3. orbit
4. path

The North Star .... page 31
1. b
2. a
3. d
4. a

Out in Space .... page 32
1. d
2. b
3. a
4. b

All in a Year .... page 33
1. Mercury has the shortest year because it orbits the sun in the least number of days. Pluto has the longest year because it orbits the sun in the greatest number of days.
2. How many Earth days is Neptune's year? Show your work.
   165 x 365 = 60,225
3. How many Earth days is Jupiter's year? Show your work.
   12 x 365 = 4,380
4. The author wrote the article to tell how long a year lasts on each planet.

I Want to Be a Knight .... page 34
1. b
2. d
3. c
4. a

Tool Time .... pages 35–36
1. d
2. b
3. b
4. c
5. b
6. a
7. c
8. a

The Farming Life .... page 37
1. Eight oxen are needed to pull the plow.
2. The lord of the castle protects the farmers from danger. The farmers work to pay for the service.
3. The farmers work at the castle, shear sheep, and repair their homes.
4. Possible answer: Animals cost a lot of money to keep. Few farmers have plows. They share these things so they can get their work done and have time to do other things.

Castles .... page 38
1. city
2. treasure
3. lord
4. food or grocery

Catherine Helps .... page 39
1. A loom is a tool used to weave.
2. She combed the fleece to remove the tangles and dirt.
3. The fleece was put on a distaff and made into yarn.
4. Wool cloth was made from the fleece of sheep.

Answer Key

A Farming Experiment .... page 40
1. The crops were not as rich and healthy as they had been.
2. They planted some crops in the spring and some crops in the fall.
3. They divided their field into three parts and let one part go unplanted for one year.
4. The farmers divided their fields into three parts. They only planted two parts each year. A different part of the field would rest. They rotated which part would rest so that after three years, each of the parts had a chance to rest.

What Fun! .... page 41
1. Possible answer: Minstrels were people who entertained long ago. They traveled to different towns to tell stories, sing songs, dance, and play musical instruments.
2. Minstrels received food and a place to stay as their pay.
3. Possible answer: Minstrels used the same songs, dances, and stories. The people watching the show would get tired of seeing the same show, so they went to new places where others had not seen their act.
4. An actor tells stories and sings songs to entertain people, just like minstrels.

This Is an Acre .... page 42
1. An acre was shaped like a rectangle.
2.
```
              220 feet
         ┌──────────────┐
22 feet  │              │ 22 feet
         └──────────────┘
              220 feet
```
3. The length was chosen by how long th oxen could work before resting – 220 feet (67m). The width was determined by a rod, a tool peasants used to make the oxen move. The width was set at four times the rod length—22 feet (7m).
4. Answers will vary.

Marco Polo Returns .... pages 43-44
1. Marco had been gone 24 years.
2. The khan sent Marco to talk to the people in the kingdom and gave Marco many treasures as payment.
3. The Khan did not want him to leave.
4. The money in China was printed on paper, while the money in Italy was made of metal.
5. Writing each page by hand took long hours. A book would take months to complete. A machine that printed pictures could probably be used to print words, too. Books would not need to be printed by hand anymore.
6. The postal system has stations that are like the places where the messengers lived. A letter goes to many different stations before it reaches the person to whom it is addressed.

Join a Guild .... page 45
1. A merchant bought and sold goods.
2. Possible answer: Goods are things people can buy and sell.
3. Merchants who sold the same kind of goods could join a guild.
4. Possible answer: Buyers would want the cheaper price. No one would buy from the guild. Then the guild would have to lower the price of its goods.

Children Help, Too .... page 46
1. Possible answer: Daniel is older because he must do a harder kind of math. Millie only has to write the alphabet.
2. Both children had to keep the fire going, milk the cow, and do school work.
3. Possible answer: Girls did work like their mothers. They helped in the kitchen, watched younger children, and sewed. Boys did work like their fathers. They helped with the animals and worked in the field.

Answer Key

Landforms on the Oregon Trail .... pages 47–48
1. d
2. c
3. a
4. c
5. b
6. a
7. d

You're Invited to a House-Raising .... pages 49–50
1. It is summer. The article talks about the fall and winter months coming and Mr. Jackson felling trees in the spring.
2. Possible answer: Pioneers needed a place to live. They used the things that they could easily find to make a cover to keep the sun and rain off.
3. Finding mud, clay, and moss was easy work and did not take much strength. The women and children could be doing this work while the men were doing the heavier work with the logs.
4. Drawing should show 20 feet long, 16 feet wide, and 7 feet high.
5. Possible answer: The people had worked together to complete a home. They were happy about it. Also, settlers did not often get to spend time with their neighbors. A barn raising was a time to play.
6. Possible answer: Building a home was hard work for one family. Homes needed to be built quickly to protect the people.

Johnnycakes .... page 51
1. c
2. d
3. c
4. a

Packing for the Trip .... page 52
1. 600 + 10 + 100 + 1,080 + 50 + 75 + 10 + 150 + 5 = 2,080 lbs.
2. $30.00 + $1.00 + $8.00 + $20.00 + $3.00 + $3.75 + $1.00 + $7.00 + $2.75 = $76.50
3. $1.00 x 75 = $75.00

Kitchen Music .... page 53
1. kitchens
2. spoons
3. jug
4. washboard

Problems on the Plains .... page 54
1. The Native Americans were angry because of settlers farming on the plain and the railroad.
2. Buffalo were killed because they were used for food for the railroad workers or for their hides.
3. Most likely answer: They wanted the land for the settlers.

Life in a Desert .... pages 55–56
1. a
2. c
3. b
4. a
5. D
6. It is so hot during the day that animals stay under the ground where it is cooler. They come out when it is not so hot. Also, if animals moved around in the heat, they would need to drink more water.

Pioneer Troubles .... pages 57–58
1. Homesteaders got free land by working on it for five years.
2. A settler who claimed land and worked on it for five years.
3. The settlers could not build homes, make fences, or make fires because there were no trees on the plains.
4. Settlers could make fences with barbed wire. They were able to raise cattle to help them earn money and to live.
5. The windmill helped them keep their crops healthy by providing water.

Answer Key

A Cloth Picture ....pages 59–60
1. Possible answer: They take skill to make, and they are pictures.
2. Possible answer: They used the quilts to pack dishes, for warmth, and for keeping rain out of the house.
3. Answers will vary.
4. The family may have just raised a barn.
5. There was little time to get together with friends, so it was time to do work as well as get together with friends.
6. Answers will vary.

Why Animals Can't Talk ....page 61–62
1. Yes, the people trust Dog because he takes care of their children.
2. Most likely answer: As the people grew in number, they needed more food. They hunted and fished in the same places as Wolf and Beaver. The people were taking the food that Wolf and Beaver needed.
3. The Great Spirit takes away the animals' speech after he arrives.
4. Answers will vary.

Pookie's Walk ....pages 63–64
1. b
2. d
3. a
4. c
5. Answers will vary. Check details of map with story.

Caring for Speckles.......................page 65
1. c
2. d
3. a
4. b

Aquarium Competition ....page 66
1. a
2. b
3. b
4. Possible answer: A bully is someone who is mean to somebody weaker.

Small, Medium, and Large Dogs ....page 67
1. The largest dog is the mastiff, and it can weigh up to 185 pounds.
2. The weight difference is 65 pounds.
3. The order is pekingese, labrador retriever, and mastiff.
4. The author wrote this article to tell about the services a store offers.

An Unusual Pet ....page 68
1. reptile
2. pets
3. skin
4. attention

Pet Survey ....pages 69–70
1. Six students have fish.
2. More students have cats than any other pets.
3. Four more students have dogs than birds.
4.

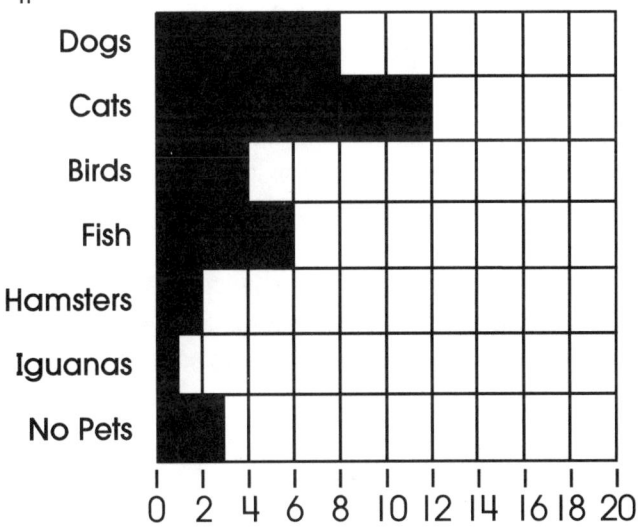

Answer Key

Pet Pictures .... page 71
1. a
2. d
3. b
4. b

The Speech .... page 72
1. Possible answer: He was working to make the world a better place to live.
2. Macaws are becoming extinct because people are catching large numbers of the birds to sell as pets. There are few macaws left in Brazil.
3. Julio wrote the speech to get students to raise money to help the macaws.
4. Possible answer: Julio was nervous because he was going to give a speech to the students in his school, asking for their help on a project. Julio probably felt relieved after he finished his speech.

Three-Dimensional Buildings .. pages 73–74
1. The story is about the three-dimensional shapes of buildings.
2. A three-dimensional shape is a figure that has space and takes up volume.
3. Rectangular prism, pyramid, cone, sphere, dome.
4. Possible answer: A cube is formed with six squares, and a rectangular prism is formed with four rectangles and two squares.
5. A dome is like a sphere with a flat base.
6. Drawings will vary.

Snow Today, Water Tomorrow! .... page 75
1. b
2. c
3. d
4. a

Building Artists .... page 76
1. An architect plans and draws pictures of what houses look like.
2. An architect and an artist both make pictures. They think about color, shape, and style.
3. An architect uses a computer to draw the final building plans.
4. The author will probably go to the library to draw on the computer.

Kinds of Houses .... page 77
1. clay
2. grass
3. trees
4. tent

House Patterns .... page 78
1. a
2. one-dimensional polygons
3. b
4. Answers will vary.

The Japanese House .... page 79
1. *Traditional* means customs that have been passed down in families.
2. The floor might get wet, and the house might get cold.
3. The people want to keep the mats in good shape and show good manners.
4. Answers will vary.

That's Electricity .... page 80
1. b
2. a
3. d
4. c

Julie's Budget .... page 81
1. A budget is a plan to spend money.
2. Julie planned to save $5.
3. She planned to spend $3 more.
4. Answers will vary.

Answer Key

Time to Vote ....page 82
1. responsibility
2. We should choose a person who makes good decisions because he or she will lead the country.
3. Gino helps his classmates and helps Mr. West with his lawn.
4. Answers will vary.

Growing Up ....page 83
1. The author wrote to tell her dad about the photos saw of him while he was growing up.
2. She wrote about the stages of a baby, a toddler, a child, a teenager, and an adult.
3. The main characters are Dad and Grandma.
4. Answers will vary.

The Family Portrait ....page 84
1. Carla was in a place where a person uses a camera to take photographs.
2. A portrait is a picture of people.
3. Portraits today are photographs. Portraits long ago were painted.
4. Possible answer: Carla decided that waiting for several minutes was better than standing still for several hours at a time in the same position, as people did long ago to have their portrait painted.

Happy Kwanzaa! ....page 85
1. The story is mostly about the history and customs of the African-American holiday Kwanzaa.
2. Possible answers: People think about family, African traditions, ways to help in the community, and the fact that Kwanzaa is a harvest celebration in Africa.
3. The items set on the table were corn and fruit, foods that would be harvested. Also, the mat was made out of straw, another material that could be harvested.
4. A kinara holds seven candles.

David Goes to Work ....page 86
1. David wanted to buy his mother a necklace for her birthday.
2. David needed $6.73 more: $15.00 − $8.27 = $6.73.
3. David will not have enough. He will be $0.23 short: $2.00 + $0.50 + $4.00 = $6.50; $6.50 +$8.27 = $14.77; $15.00 - $14.77 = $0.23.

The Totem Pole ....page 87
1. The author wrote this article to get people to British Columbia, Canada.
2. Answers will vary.
3. Answers will vary.
4. They gave gifts.

A Family ....page 88
1. a
2. b
3. b
4. d

Mr. Nobody ....page 89
1. Possible answer: The make-believe person is the one who takes the blame for bad things that happen in the house.
2. He shows up when bad things happen.
3. The person would not want to get into trouble.
4. Answers will vary.

Many Kinds of Communities ....page 90
1. Possible answer: Both communities have things that are needed to live.
2. Possible answer: People who sing could be in a music community. They could go to concerts together.
3. Possible answer: A fish could belong to an ocean community.
4. The author wrote the article to tell about the different kinds of communities.

An Ant Community ....page 91
1. a
2. d
3. d
4. a

© McGraw-Hill Children's Publishing   0-7424-1923-1 *Theme-Based Reading Comprehension*

Answer Key

It's the Law .... page 92
1. law
2. mayor
3. council
4. community

A Chain of Life .... pages 93-94
1. c
2. d
3. b
4. d
5. b
6. A food chain can be broken if a member gets sick or if a member's numbers decrease for some reason.

Community Fun .... page 95
1. b
2. d
3. b
4. d

Vacation Weather .... page 96
1. Possible answer: No, it is still too cold.
2. Possible answer: No, you could not ski because the weather is too warm for the snow to stay on the ground.
3. Possible answer: Yes, the weather is pleasant.
4. Answers will vary.

The Mural Contest .... page 97
1. A mural is a large painted picture.
2. Possible answer: It would be something bright to look at, and it would cover up something that was old.
3. People can draw a picture of an idea they have for a mural, or they can help paint the mural.
4. Answers will vary.

Communities Here and There ...... page 98
1. It is probably in the city.
2. Answers will vary, but may reflect that the writing on th building is not in English.
3. Answers will vary, but may include tall buildings, trees, people, sidewalks, and so on.
4. Answers will vary.

Why Bears Hibernate in Winter: A Native-American Folktale .... pages 99-100
1. Bear boasted about being the biggest, strongest, fastest animal in the woods.
2. The animals wanted Turtle to win so Bear would stop bragging.
3. Elk yelled for the race to begin after he punched holes in the ice.
4. Bear left the race because he could not win. He did not want to face the other animals.
5. Turtle won the race because someone in his family was by each hole. They took turns looking up through the holes.
6. Possible answer: No, Turtle did not win fairly because he did not swim the whole way by himself.
7. Possible answer: No, Bear will not boast anymore because he is too embarrassed about being beaten by a little turtle.

The March Wind .... page 101
1. The poem tells what the wind is doing at the end of winter and the beginning of spring.
2. Possible answer: It tosses the leaves into the air and blows the children around.
3. The wind blows across the ground that is still frozen from winter.
4. The last line says that it wakes the flowers from sleep, which is a sign of spring.

How Far Away? .... page 102
1. Thunder happens at the same time lightning strikes.
2. Thunder cannot be heard if it is more than 10 miles away.
3. The thunderstorm was 4,800 feet away: 1,200 x 4 = 4,800 feet.
4. The storm was less than a mile away: 4,800 < 5,200.

Make a Tornado .... page 103
1. d
2. c
3. a
4. a

Answer Key

Ellie's Favorite Season .... page 104
1. Baseball season begins in April.
2. The baseball season ends in October because that is when the playoffs are held to determine the winner of the pennant.
3. Beth plays baseball because she says she is glad her team only plays 30 games in a season.
4. The author wanted to tell a funny story.
5. Possible answer: Football season and basketball season are two other sports seasons.

Animals Adapt .... page 105
1. It probably rains a lot during the wet season in Africa.
2. Some animals adapt by slowing down their breathing and their heartbeat.
3. A lungfish breathes air.
4. Possible answer: They do not move so they do not need food or water.

Monsoon Winds .... page 106
1. monsoon
2. summer
3. rain
4. dry

The Climate Seasons .... page 107
1. a
2. d
3. b
4. c

Gung Hay Fat Choy! .... page 108
1. People wish others a happy and wealthy year.
2. Students choose three: buy presents, paint windows and doors red, clean their houses, make special food, or buy new clothes.
3. The people eat special food with family and friends, and they watch fireworks.
4. Answers will vary.

Insects—One Big Happy Group .... page 109
1. d
2. c
3. c
4. b

Insect Record Holders .... page 110
1. This story is real because it gives facts about animals and humans. It is make-believe because an ant is talking.
2. Answers will vary. Students multiply their weight times 30.
3. Humans would have to jump half a mile into the air.
4. Answers will vary. Students multiply their weight times 50.

Silk-Screen Prints .... page 111
1. woodblock and silk-screen
2. In woodblock printing, the design is cut into the wood and then printed on paper. In silk-screen printing, the design is made by cutting shapes out of paper and placing them on the paper to be printed. Ink is pressed through the silk cloth to cover the shapes.
3. The printer uses a rubber blade to squeeze the ink through the silk.
4. If the screen is not washed, the new ink color will mix with the old ink color. The colors will be different than expected.

Big Bugs .... page 112
1. gnat
2. small
3. wet
4. walking stick

Butterfly Lessons .... page 113
1. Penny did not like math because she said math was boring.
2. Possible answer: Penny probably knew the Monarch butterfly was orange and black.
3. The color and line pattern on the wings were the same on each side.
4. Penny will probably continue to do her homework outside because she opened her math book again.

Answer Key

A New Kind of Thermometer ......page 114
1. c
2. b
3. a
4. a

A Butterfly Life Cycle ....page 115
1. A life cycle is the growth pattern of a living thing that happens over and over again.
2. It needs the food because it grows so quickly.
3. a. egg
   b. larva
   c. pupa
   d. adult

The Legend of Silk ....page 116
1. The king called his wife and asked her to find out what had happened to the tree.
2. The worms were eating the leaves of a mulberry tree.
3. The boiling water caused the cocoon to spread apart.

Working to Save the Monarch Butterfly ....page 117
1. *Migrate* means to move from one place to another.
2. The forest is in danger because loggers are cutting down trees.
3. The government has passed laws to protect the butterflies and has turned more land into parks. They also pay people who lose their logging jobs.
4. When people learn about the problems, they are more willing to help.